ACCUPLACER ESL LOEP PRACTICE TESTS & ESL LOEP STUDY GUIDE

ADVANTAGE+ EDITION

Note: Accuplacer is a registered trademark of the College Board, which is neither affiliated with nor endorses this publication.

Accuplacer ESL LOEP Practice Tests and ESL LOEP Study Guide Advantage Plus Edition

© COPYRIGHT 1995, 2016 Academic Success Media © COPYRIGHT 2020 Academic Success Group.

All rights reserved. No part of this publication may be reproduced, stored in a retrieval system, or transmitted, in any form or by any means, electronic, mechanical, photocopying, recording, or otherwise.

ISBN: 978-1-949282-56-6

COPYRIGHT NOTICE TO EDUCATORS: Please respect copyright law. Under no circumstances may you make copies of these materials for distribution to or use by students. Should you wish to use the materials with students, you are required to purchase a copy of this publication for each of your students.

Note: Accuplacer is a registered trademark of the College Board, which is neither affiliated with nor endorses this publication.

TABLE OF CONTENTS

Accuplacer ESL LOEP Practice Test 1:
    Reading Skills Test 1   1
    Language Usage Test 1   7
    Sentence Meaning Test 1   10

Accuplacer ESL LOEP Practice Test 2:
    Reading Skills Test 2   13
    Language Usage Test 2   20
    Sentence Meaning Test 2   22

Accuplacer ESL LOEP Practice Test 3:
    Reading Skills Test 3   25
    Language Usage Test 3   31
    Sentence Meaning Test 3   34

Answers to the Practice Tests   37

Accuplacer ESL LOEP Study Guide:

    Verb tense and form   40
    Comparatives and Superlatives   41
    Conditional Sentences   42
    Gerunds and Infinitives   43
    Misplaced Modifiers   47
    Restrictive and Non-restrictive Modifiers   47
    The "Negative Inversion" Sentence Structure   48
    Using Past Participle Phrases   48
    Past Perfect Tense   49
    Punctuation and Independent Clauses   49
    Punctuation and Quotation Marks   50
    Sentence Linking Phrases and Subordination   50

    Grammar Exercise 1: Negative Adverbial Clauses   55
    Grammar Exercise 2: Past Perfect   58
    Grammar Exercise 3: Prepositions   59
    Grammar Exercise 4: Review of Gerunds and Infinitives   61
    Grammar Exercise 5: "So" and "Such"   63
    Grammar Exercise 6: Phrasal Verbs – Part 1   64
    Grammar Exercise 7: The Definite Article – "The"   67
    Grammar Exercise 8: Comparatives and Superlatives   69
    Grammar Exercise 9: The Third Conditional   71
    Grammar Exercise 10: Phrasal Verbs – Part 2   73

    Answers to the Grammar Exercises   76

    Accuplacer ESL LOEP Idiom List   82

    Reading Comprehension Tips   89

    Essay Topics   90

ADVANTAGE PLUS EDITION BONUS MATERIAL

ADDITIONAL GRAMMAR REVIEW AND PRACTICE EXERCISES

Adverbs of Place – Location	92
Exercises – Adverbs of Location	95
Adverbs of Degree	96
Exercises – Adverbs of Degree	98
Another / Other / Others	99
Exercises – Another / Other / Others – Exercises	100
Emphatic Form with Do and Did	101
Exercises – Emphatic Form (Do and Did)	102
Modal Verbs	103
Exercises – Modal Verbs	105
Perfect Infinitive	106
Exercises – Perfect Infinitive	108
Pronouns in the Accusative Case	109
Exercises – Pronouns in the Accusative Case	110
Pronouns – Demonstrative and Relative Pronouns	111
Exercises – Demonstrative and Relative Pronouns	113
Review of Verb Usage and Tense	114
Grammar Review Exercises – Set 1	122
Grammar Review Exercises – Set 2	125
Grammar Review Exercises – Set 3	128
Answers to the Bonus Exercises	131

HOW TO USE THIS PUBLICATION

The Accuplacer ESL LOEP (Levels of English Proficiency) examination contains three parts: reading skills, language usage, and sentence meaning.

The study guide in the second part of this book reviews the aspects of grammar and language that are covered on the actual Accuplacer ESL test.

The study guide also explains the types of questions that students are likely to encounter on the reading skills section of the test and gives tips for answering these types of questions.

Most students will therefore find it beneficial to review the material in the study guide in the second part of this book, as well as the bonus exercises at the end of the book, before attempting the practice tests in the first part of the book.

The first part of this publication contains three complete Accuplacer ESL practice tests.

If you simply want to get acquainted with the format of the test and to practice for the exam, you can begin at the start of the book and try the practice tests.

The answers for the practice tests are included at the end of practice test 3.

Students may also be asked to write an essay as part of the Accuplacer.

If you need further help with essay writing, you may be interested in our other publication entitled:

Writeplacer Success: Accuplacer Essay Writing Guide

ACCUPLACER ESL LOEP – PRACTICE TEST 1

Reading Skills: For this section, you will read short passages and answer questions about them. Some questions will be about information which you can find directly in the passage. For other questions, you must make inferences from what you have read.

1. Recent research shows that the rise in teenage smoking in the 1990s primarily took place in youth from more affluent families, whose parents were both working. Therefore, these teenagers were not from disadvantaged homes, as most people seem to believe. In fact, the facts demonstrate quite the opposite because the most striking and precipitous rise in smoking was for teenagers from the most financially advantageous backgrounds.

   What is the primary purpose of this passage?

   A. to provide information on a recent trend
   B. to emphasize the dangers of smoking
   C. to dispel a common misconception
   D. to highlight the difference between two types of teenagers

2. When Americans are bored or restless, an easy solution is readily available: simply turn on the television. One thing for certain is that we have an overabundance of television programs available to us. Today Americans have three national networks and a plethora of digital channels from which to choose.

   Television programs:

   A. are few and far between.
   B. are broadcast during purchased airtime.
   C. are constantly being altered.
   D. provide Americans with more than enough options.

3. Gene splicing, the process whereby a small part of the DNA of one organism is removed and inserted into the DNA chain of another organism, has produced results like the super tomato. In order to create the super tomato, the gene resistant to cold temperatures on the DNA chain of a particular type of cold-water fish was isolated, removed, and inserted into an ordinary tomato plant. This resulted in a new type of tomato plant that can thrive in cold weather conditions.

   From this passage, it seems safe to conclude that:

   A. the super tomato was the first case of gene splicing.
   B. the super tomato is only one example of gene splicing.
   C. DNA from tomatoes has also been inserted into certain types of fish.
   D. Many people object to gene splicing.

4. Working parents have recently prompted widespread growth in the American educational system. It is now common for children from both middle class and well-to-do families to begin nursery school at the age of two. Most parents also take advantage of the opportunity to send their children to pre-school after nursery school. Neither of these educational programs, which are operated independently by private organizations, is mandatory. In fact, state-sponsored education is not usually compulsory until the child is five years old.

Nursery and pre-school programs:

A. are required by the state government.
B. are operated only by charities.
C. are attended by children from various economic levels of society.
D. have developed slowly over time.

5. In 1804, Meriwether Lewis and William Clark began an expedition across the western United States, then known as the Louisiana Territory. The two men had met years earlier and established a long-lasting friendship. When Lewis was later a young captain in the army, he received a letter from President Thomas Jefferson offering him funding to explore the Western country. With Jefferson's permission, Lewis offered a partnership in the expedition to his friend Clark. When their journey had safely concluded 8,000 miles later, the pair had made many crucial discoveries about our nation.

The purpose of the passage is:

A. to give the background to Lewis and Clark's westward expedition
B. to defend the purchase of the Louisiana Territory
C. to state a crucial decision made by Thomas Jefferson
D. to compare the skills of Lewis and Clark

6. The American Civil War, one of the most pivotal chapters in American history, was marked by the secession of the southern states from the Union. After this divergence, two new nations were formed. The northern states, whose residents were called Yankees, continued to be known as the United States of America. Their adversaries in the southern states, the Confederates, had consolidated and called themselves the Confederate States of America. Although the draft was yet not in existence, many young men enlisted voluntarily after the war had started.

The American Civil War began:

A. when the Yankees established a new nation.
B. because the draft had not been created at that time.
C. when young men joined the army voluntarily.
D. when the Confederate states separated from the northern states.

7. The Watergate burglary had many aspects, but at its center was President Richard Nixon. Throughout the investigation of the burglary, government officials denied involvement in the crime. An extensive cover-up operation followed in an attempt to conceal those who were involved in planning the break-in. This subterfuge failed when the FBI investigated the one-hundred-dollar bills that were found in the pockets of the burglars. After making inquiries, the FBI discovered that this money originated from the Committee for the Re-election of the President, thereby confirming governmental involvement. In the end, individuals who had entered the highest branches of the government to serve and protect the people went to prison instead.

    What is main reason why the cover-up of the Watergate break-in failed?

    A. because the Committee for the Re-election of the President denied involvement
    B. because of the subterfuge of the FBI
    C. because the burglars' money was traced back to a governmental organization
    D. because its ringleaders went to prison

8. The first step in making a major motion picture is to obtain the movie script, which is usually procured from the Screen Writers' Guild. Since the strength of the story can make or break the production, movies with underdeveloped or disjointed plots are automatically refused. The next step is to find a producer who is capable of winning the financial endowment of a major motion picture company for the movie's production. Companies such as Touchstone and Paramount are currently among the forerunners in the motion picture production industry.

    Which statement is true according to the passage?

    A. The movie script must originate from the Screen Writers' Guild.
    B. Productions of stories with intricate plots will receive only minimal monetary support from the motion picture company.
    C. The producer is responsible for winning financial backing from the motion picture company.
    D. Touchstone and Paramount are the best motion picture companies in Hollywood.

9. Organic farming has become one of the fastest growing trends in agriculture recently. Over the past ten years, sales of organic products in the United States have increased a staggering twenty percent, with retail sales per year of more than nine billion dollars. American farmers have realized that organic farming is an incredibly cost-effective method because it can potentially be used to control costs, as well as to appeal to higher-priced markets. Apart from these monetary benefits, organic farming also results in positive ecological outcomes for the environment because the use of chemicals and synthetic materials is prohibited.

The main idea of the paragraph is that organic farming:

A. is a very profitable sector of the agricultural industry.
B. was less popular ten years ago.
C. prohibits chemical and synthetic materials.
D. has grown recently because it is cost-effective and environmentally-friendly.

10. When an individual driver tries to decide which new car to buy, he or she considers not only the price range of the vehicle. Personal preferences and a host of individual idiosyncrasies also come into play. Buyers classified as affluent may contemplate purchasing "town cars." Being spacious enough to seat six passengers comfortably, this automobile is seen as a status symbol that serves to flaunt the wealth of its owner.

   The kind of vehicle a consumer purchases:

   A. is determined solely by the invoice price.
   B. is mainly influenced by a particular buyer's quirks.
   C. is directly related to the customer's wealth.
   D. is influenced by a number of factors.

11. Cancer occurs when cells in the body begin to divide abnormally and form more cells without control or order. There are some factors which are known to increase the risk of cancer. Smoking is the largest single cause of death from cancer in the United States. In addition, poor food choices increase cancer risk. Indeed, research shows that there is a definite link between the consumption of high-fat food and cancer.

   From this passage, we can infer that:

   A. a low-fat diet can reduce the risk of cancer.
   B. smoking always causes cells to divide abnormally.
   C. the consumption of high-fat food has increased in recent years.
   D. most cancer sufferers have made poor food choices.

12. Many steps are required in successfully prosecuting a criminal case in the American legal system. Once the crime has been committed and discovered, the police force is dispatched to the crime scene to begin the investigation. Simultaneously, any possible suspects or witnesses are taken in for questioning at the local police precinct having jurisdiction over the case. Suspects and witnesses can be subjected to mild inquisition or full-scale interrogation, depending upon the severity of the matter.

   A criminal case in America:

   A. begins when the suspect is sued.
   B. consists of various systematic phases.
   C. is done at the local police precinct.
   D. is dependent upon the seriousness of the crime in relation to the length of questioning.

13. The theory of multiple intelligences is rapidly replacing the intelligence quotient, or IQ. The IQ, long considered the only valid way of measuring intelligence, has come under criticism recently because it inheres in many cultural biases. For this reason, there has been a movement away from the IQ test, which is now seen as an indication of a person's academic ability. On the other hand, multiple intelligence measures practical skills such as spatial, visual, and musical ability.

    The main idea of the passage is that:

    A. there are cultural biases in the IQ test.
    B. the IQ does not take true intelligence into account.
    C. the theory of multiple intelligences is generally preferable to the concept of IQ.
    D. multiple intelligence theory is a measure of an individual's practical abilities.

14. Diversification is the key to success in today's agrarian pursuits. Traditionally, farmers raised livestock such as dairy cows and flocks of sheep, allowing these herbivorous animals to graze in pastures as their primary source of feeding. Today, farmers have augmented their lines of business with the breeding of a wide range of plants and animals.

    In the past, farmers used to:

    A. raise cattle strictly for the production of beef.
    B. keep only milk-producing cows.
    C. breed only sheep and lambs.
    D. concentrate their operations on raising grass-eating animals.

15. Around the world today, more than a billion people still do not have fresh, clean drinking water available on a daily basis. Hundreds of thousands of people die needlessly every year because of the consumption of unclean, disease-ridden water. In brief, fresh water saves lives. However, what has been understood only recently is that the provision for fresh water around the globe also protects the environment because those who manage water supplies must evaluate in more detail why and how countries consume and pollute their available water. Without this evaluation, an ever-increasing number of individuals will continue to die from water-related diseases.

    We can conclude from the information in this passage that:

    A. water-related disease will decline in the future.
    B. water-related deaths could be easily avoided.
    C. children are the most vulnerable to water-related disease and death.
    D. political corruption contributes to the problem with the global water supply.

16. Vicissitudes in the political arena are predominant among the events reported by today's press. Stupendous scandals have been uncovered and covert operations foiled as a result of recent media investigations. Such discoveries often occur after immense and assiduous research into the discrepancies among various stories told by politicians. Had these duplicitous politicians been aware of the menace posed by such journalists, they would have been much more careful in carrying out their subterfuge.

    Political scandals:

    A. often come to light due to differences among various versions of stories told by politicians.
    B. are equivalent to covert operations.
    C. are rarely mentioned in the news.
    D. show the magnanimity of politicians nowadays.

17. There are many obstacles confronting recording artists wishing to make an album. If a singer, songwriter, or musician is lured by the quest for fame, he or she had better not have an aversion to hard work as seemingly insuperable snags and setbacks will often beset one's path. Nor is it a feasible notion for the artist to attempt to depend on the album royalties for his or her livelihood because success is often elusive. Musicians need to be diligent and pugnacious, and having some innate talent definitely helps as well.

    Successfully recording an album requires:

    A. a dissolute lifestyle.
    B. tenacity.
    C. an attractive personality.
    D. all of the above.

18. Sir Isaac Newton had the prescience to appreciate that his study of natural phenomena was of great import for the scientific community and for society as a whole. It is because of Newton's work that we currently understand the effect of gravity on the earth as a global system. As a result of Newton's investigation into the subject of gravity, we know today that geological features such as mountains and canyons can cause variances in the Earth's gravitational force. Newton must also be acknowledged for the realization that the force of gravity becomes less robust as the distance from the equator diminishes, due to the rotation of the earth, as well as the declining mass and density of the planet from the equator to the poles.

What is the author's main purpose?

    A. to analyze natural phenomena
    B. to reconcile various gravitational theories
    C. to identify a reservation which Newton experienced
    D. to emphasize the significance of Newton's achievement

19. The corpus of research on Antarctica has resulted in an abundance of factual data. For example, we now know that more than ninety-nine percent of the land is completely covered by snow and ice, making Antarctica the coldest continent on the planet. This inhospitable climate has brought about the adaptation of a plethora of plants and biological organisms present on the continent. An investigation into the sedimentary geological formations provides testimony to the process of adaptation. Sediments recovered from the bottom of Antarctic lakes, as well as bacteria discovered in ice, have revealed the history of climate change over the past 10,000 years.

    According to the passage, the plants and organisms in Antarctica:

        A. have survived because of the process of adaptation.
        B. are the result of sedimentary geological formations.
        C. cover more than ninety percent of the land surface.
        D. grow in the bottom of lakes on the continent.

20. A wide array of classes and workshops in the dramatic arts is available at most colleges and universities. The student may be required to attend productions at various local and regional theaters for these types of classes. Students are not merely passive members of the audience during these performances. Rather, they are expected to critique the production, noting what the actors have done well, as well as what they have done poorly.

    What are students expected to do when attending performances?

        A. passively observe
        B. practice public speaking
        C. analyze the production
        D. make suggestions for improvement

Language Usage: This section of the test assesses your knowledge of English grammar. For the first part of this section, you must choose the word or phrase that makes a grammatically correct sentence. For the second part of this section, you will see two sentences. You must then choose a grammatically correct answer from the answer choices that has the same meaning as the two sentences provided.

21. We hope _____ on vacation this Saturday.
        A. to go   C. to going
        B. going   D. to have been going

22. No sooner _____ than Alice left the party.
    A. we arrived   C. we had arrived
    B. had we arrived   D. we were arriving

23. I have never seen _____ performance.
    A. such an awful   C. so an awful
    B. such awful a   D. a so awful

24. At six feet and four inches, Jane is the _____ four sisters.
    A. tallest of the   C. taller of her
    B. taller than her   D. most tall of the

25. Bob is upset because he saw the bad accident that _____ this morning.
    A. was happening   C. happened
    B. has happened   D. happen

26. I requested that my friend _____ to the party.
    A. to be invited   C. be inviting
    B. being invited   D. be invited

27. _____ in reading popular novels.
    A. I am interesting   C. Interesting it is
    B. I am interested   D. It is interesting

28. _____ my exam today, I wanted to get a good night's sleep last night.
    A. While I have   C. Because of
    B. While having   D. Because having

29. In addition to _____ , Susan also does knitting.
    A. sew   C. she sews
    B. sewing   D. she sewing

30. My new job is going well now that I have gotten used _____ so early.
    A. to getting up   C. getting up
    B. to get up   D. get up

31. Laura loves the opera. Maria, on the other hand, hates it.
    A. Laura loves the opera. Unlike Maria, hates it.
    B. Laura loves the opera. Maria, unlike, hates it.
    C. Unlike Maria, Laura loves the opera.
    D. Unlike Laura who hates, Laura loves the opera.

32. I did not pass my exam. I did not study for it.
    A. I did not study for my exam, because of this I did not pass it.
    B. I did not study for my exam, and because of this, I did not pass it.
    C. I did not pass my exam because of I did not study for it.
    D. I did not pass my exam because of not study for it.

33. My friend put on her seatbelt. Therefore, she was not hurt in the accident.
    A. My friend would be injured in the accident had she not put on her seat belt.
    B. My friend would have been injured in the accident have she not put on her seat belt.
    C. My friend would has been injured in the accident had she not put on her seat belt.
    D. My friend would have been injured in the accident had she not put on her seat belt.

34. My mother will visit me this weekend. She will bring my brother along with her.
    A. My mother will bring my brother along with her, who will visit me this weekend.
    B. My brother along with her, my mother who will visit me this weekend.
    C. My mother, who will visit me this weekend, will bring my brother along with her.
    D. My mother, will visit me this weekend, will bring my brother along with her.

35. I like little kids. However, they must be well behaved.
    A. I like little kids, but if only they are well behaved.
    B. I like little kids, but if only are they well behaved.
    C. I like little kids, but if they only are well behaved.
    D. I like little kids, but only if they are well behaved.

36. We spent so much time talking. He told us not to do so.
    A. He was telling us not to spend so much time talking.
    B. He was telling us not to spent so much time talking.
    C. He was telling us not to spending so much time talking.
    D. He was telling us not spending so much time talking.

37. The lecture was long. Nevertheless, I managed to pay attention.
    A. Although the lecture was long, I managed to pay attention.
    B. Although the lecture was long. I managed to pay attention.
    C. Although I managed to pay attention, but the lecture was long.
    D. Although I managed to pay attention, the lecture was long.

38. Debbie has been in such a bad mood lately. She is just unbearable.
    A. Debbie has been in such a bad mood lately, that she is just unbearable.
    B. Debbie has been in such a bad mood lately, so she is just unbearable.
    C. Debbie has been in such a bad mood lately, which she is just unbearable.
    D. Debbie has been in such a bad mood lately, who is just unbearable.

39. He lost his job. It often happens to people.
    A. Often happens, he lost his job.
    B. As often happens, he lost his job.
    C. It often happens, he lost his job.
    D. So often happens, he lost his job.

40. I saw Grant Wood's paintings. They were in the museum.
    A. I saw in the museum Grant Wood's paintings.
    B. While in the museum, I saw Grant Wood's paintings.
    C. In the museum, Grant Wood's paintings where I saw them.
    D. Grant Wood's paintings, they were in the museum where I saw them.

Sentence Meaning: This section tests your knowledge of English vocabulary. For the first part of this section, you must choose the correct word to fill in the gap in the sentence provided. For the second part of this section, you will read sentences that contain idioms. You must then choose the answer that best explains the idiom provided.

41. The store specializes in formal _____ for men and women, including suits and dresses.
    A. apparel C. whims
    B. fads D. enterprises

42. The media's emphasis on health and fitness has caused many new gyms to spring _____ .
    A. out C. up
    B. around D. forward

43. The ceremony _____ at 9:00 am and lasts until 11:00 am.
    A. compels C. prompts
    B. commences D. fetters

44. John was _____ when his job application was rejected.
    A. demoralized C. lauded
    B. invigorated D. flanked

45. A lot of cotton is _____ in the southern states, particularly Georgia.
    A. underdeveloped C. contravened
    B. refrained D. produced

46. _____ with others is essential for effective teamwork.
    A. Disposition C. Extravagance
    B. Procurement D. Cooperation

47. The vacation in the Bahamas that they had planned failed to _____ .
    A. contrive C. endow
    B. refrain D. materialize

48. This machine has a _____ which prevents it from functioning properly.
    A. defect C. fume
    B. fabric D. chassis

49. He is currently being _____ for armed robbery.
    A. dispatched C. suspected
    B. prosecuted D. subjected

50. The United Nations volunteers were sent out on a _____ to the famine area in Africa.
    A. refectory C. defile
    B. mission D. tenet

51. It has grown by leaps and bounds.

    The speaker means that:
    A. It has grown dramatically.
    B. It has grown superficially.
    C. It has grown marginally.
    D. It has surpassed its boundaries.

52. The president gave the go-ahead.

    What did the president do?
    A. He started doing something.
    B. He gave money.
    C. He gave permission.
    D. He acquiesced.

53. It was his undoing.

    The speaker means that:
    A. it caused him to change.
    B. it caused him to reassess the situation.
    C. it led to new events.
    D. it led to his downfall.

54. Did they bring him around?

    The speaker is asking whether:
    A. he came along with them.
    B. he delivered something to them.
    C. they solved his problems.
    D. they were able to change his mind.

55. I decided to bail out of it.

    The speaker is saying that she:
    A. decided not to continue doing something.
    B. had to remove water from something.
    C. had to take something off.
    D. had to spend too much money on something.

56. The results hinge upon that happening.

    The results:
    A. depend on something else.
    B. rely on someone else.
    C. are unpredictable.
    D. are unreliable.

57. His friend told him off.

    What did his friend do?
    A. told him a secret.
    B. scolded him.
    C. spoke to him.
    D. lied to him.

58. Can you pick me up?

    The speaker is asking for:
    A. a delivery.
    B. a collection.
    C. a ride.
    D. encouragement.

59. I can't make heads or tails of this.

    The speaker can't:
    A. believe in it.
    B. understand it.
    C. change it.
    D. translate it.

60. My friend will stand up for me.

    What will the friend do for the speaker?
    A. defend her
    B. help her
    C. lift her up
    D. encourage her

ACCUPLACER ESL LOEP – PRACTICE TEST 2

Reading Skills: For this section, you will read short passages and answer questions about them. Some questions will be about information which you can find directly in the passage. For other questions, you must make inferences from what you have read.

1. Our ability to measure brain activity is owing to the research of two European scientists. It was in 1929 that electrical activity in the human brain was first discovered. Hans Berger, the German psychiatrist who made the discovery, was despondent to find out, however, that many other scientists quickly dismissed his research. The work of Berger was confirmed three years later when Edgar Adrian, a Briton, clearly demonstrated that the brain, like the heart, is profuse in its electrical activity. Because of Adrian's work, we know that the electrical impulses in the brain, called brain waves, are a mixture of four different frequencies.

    The purpose of the passage is to describe:

    A. two opposing theories.
    B. important research about brain activity.
    C. a personal opinion about the work of two scientists.
    D. the different types of brain wave frequencies.

2. The hatching of fish is a highly delicate process and must be monitored carefully. The scales, or skin of the fish, must be examined to ensure that they are of the correct color and consistency. The gills must also be looked at to determine whether the fish can breathe freely. Additionally, the fins must be scrutinized to determine whether the fish is able to swim properly.

    Fish must be examined to ensure that:

    A. they can inhale and exhale properly through their gills.
    B. their scales are fit for the purpose of respiration.
    C. their fins are the proper shade and texture.
    D. All of the above.

3. In the Black Hills, four visages protrude from the side of a mountain. The faces are those of four United States' presidents: George Washington, Thomas Jefferson, Theodore Roosevelt, and Abraham Lincoln. Washington was chosen on the basis of being the first president. Jefferson was instrumental in the writing of the American Declaration of Independence. Lincoln was selected on the basis of the mettle he demonstrated during the American Civil War, and Roosevelt for his development of Square Deal policy, as well as being a proponent of the construction of the Panama Canal.

From this passage, it seems reasonable to assume that these four presidents were chosen for the monument because:

A. of their outstanding courage.
B. their faces would be esthetically sympathetic to the natural surroundings.
C. they helped to improve the national economy.
D. their work was considered crucial to the progress of the nation.

4. The nation has seen an increase in publicized knife crimes recently, with many front-page newspaper stories devoted to the latest victim of another vicious attack. Last summer, for instance, a twenty-two-year-old man was stabbed in Central Park in yet another high-profile case. While media attention has increased dramatically in the last few years, the actual figures show that knife crime has remained reasonably constant at around seven to eight percent of all crime. However, these figures will do little to appease the victims of the stabbings and knife attacks that have made the news headlines.

The writer suggests that members of the public may view knife crime as an exigent social problem primarily because:

A. more newspaper publicity has been devoted to knife crimes recently.
B. a man was stabbed recently in Central Park.
C. it is difficult to deal with the victims of the attacks.
D. knife crime has increased dramatically in recent years.

5. The student readiness educational model is based on the view that that students are individuals, each operating at different levels of ability. For some students, this might mean that they are operating above the average ability level of their contemporaries, while others may be functioning at a level that is below average. There are also students who are learning at the optimum level because they are being challenged and learning new things, but yet they do not feel overwhelmed or inundated by the new information. According to the student readiness approach, the onus falls on teachers to create classroom learning activities that will challenge the maximum number of students.

This passage is primarily about:

A. the rationale of one particular educational method.
B. the individuality of various students.
C. the burdens placed on teachers.
D. the shortcomings of teachers and students.

6. Highly concentrated radioactive waste is lethal and can remain so for thousands of years. Accordingly, the disposal of this material remains an issue in most energy-producing countries around the world. Rather than being disposed of, liquid forms of radioactive waste are usually stored in stainless steel tanks. The long-term problem lies in the fact that nuclear waste generates heat as the radioactive atoms decay. This excess heat could ultimately result in a radioactive leak. Therefore, the liquid needs to be cooled by pumping cold water into coils inside the tanks. This means that the tanks are only a temporary storage solution. The answer to the long term storage of nuclear waste may be fusing the waste into glass cylinders that are stored deep underground.

Why is the process of pumping cold water into the coils mentioned in the passage?

A. to highlight the fact that radioactive waste is lethal
B. to explain how potential radioactive leaks are averted
C. to compare different methods for storing radioactive waste
D. to predict how radioactive waste will be handled in the future

7. Socio-economic status, rather than intellectual ability, may be the key to a child's success later in life. Consider two hypothetical elementary school students named John and Paul. Both of these children work hard, pay attention in the classroom, and are respectful to their teachers. Yet, Paul's father is a prosperous business tycoon, while John's has a menial job working in a factory. Despite the similarities in their academic aptitudes, the disparate economic situations of their parents means that Paul is nearly thirty times more likely than John to land a high-flying job by the time he reaches his fortieth year. In fact, John has only a twelve percent chance of finding and maintaining a job that would earn him even a median-level income.

We can conclude from information in this passage that:

A. academic ability is directly related to one's financial status later in life.
B. children from high-income families are academically successful.
C. children from affluent families are more likely to remain affluent as they grow older.
D. most children from low-income families will get jobs in factories.

8. Stories about the exploration of the American frontier have become more popular than fables or nursery rhymes. Perhaps the popularity of these tales is owing to the mystery surrounding them. It is difficult for us to fathom how these hearty pioneers defied the odds in spite of the exceptionally precarious conditions they faced.

Stories about the American West:

A. have been superseded many times.
B. are totally incomprehensible.
C. have not become unpopular over the years.
D. are generally misconstrued.

9. The most significant characteristic of any population is its age-sex structure, defined as the proportion of people of each gender in each different age group. The age-sex structure determines the potential for reproduction, and therefore population growth. Thus, the age-sex structure has social policy implications. For instance, a population with a high proportion of elderly citizens needs to consider its governmentally-funded pension schemes and health care systems carefully. Conversely, a greater percentage of young children in the population might imply that educational funding and child welfare policies need to be evaluated. Accordingly, as the composition of a population changes over time, the government may need to re-evaluate its funding priorities.

   Governmental funding decisions should primarily be based on:

   A. the composition of the age and gender of its population.
   B. the number of elderly citizens in its population.
   C. the percentage of children in its population.
   D. social policy limitations.

10. In today's hectic times, most people are too busy even to grab a bite for lunch. However, this is not the case on Thanksgiving Day, for this is the day not only to give thanks for bountiful blessings, but also to indulge. Indeed, Thanksgiving Day is the day to eat. The preparation of the Thanksgiving Day meal entails many details, including the accommodation of any special dietary requests. Therefore, the cook had better get to the supermarket early to avoid rummaging through the larder at the last minute.

    Thanksgiving Day celebration consists of:

    A. a quick bite to eat.
    B. only a few morsels.
    C. a variety of confections and refreshments.
    D. a dearth of food.

11. Earthquakes occur when there is motion in the tectonic plates on the surface of the earth. The crust of the earth contains twelve such tectonic plates, which are from four to ten kilometers in length when located below the sea, although those on land can be from thirty to seventy kilometers long. Fault lines, the places where these plates meet, build up a great deal of pressure because the plates are constantly pressing on each other. So, the two plates will eventually shift or separate because the pressure on them is constantly increasing, and this build-up of energy needs to be released. When the plates shift or separate, we have an occurrence of an earthquake, also known as a seismic event.

    The main purpose of the passage is:

    A. to investigate a geological theory.
    B. to describe the events that result in a natural phenomenon.
    C. to propose a solution to a problem.
    D. to provide background to a personal observation.

12. Advertising companies will reach the largest audience during what is known as "Prime Time," the window of advertising opportunity from 7:00 pm. to 10:00 pm. Taking the volume of television viewers into account, commercial entities devour this airtime with alacrity. Other commercial opportunities exist during morning and afternoon broadcasts of long-running talk shows, game shows, and soap operas, which are now euphemistically called "daytime dramas."

    Advertisers will communicate their messages to the largest amount of viewers:

    A. during talk shows.
    B. during the evening hours.
    C. in the morning.
    D. in the afternoon.

13. The Hong Kong and Shanghai Bank Corporation (HSBC) skyscraper in Hong Kong is one of the world's most famous high-rise buildings. The building was designed so that it had many pre-built parts that were not constructed on site. This prefabrication made the project a truly international effort: the windows were manufactured in Austria, the exterior walls were fabricated in the United States, the toilets and air-conditioning were made in Japan, and many of the other components came from Germany.

    The main idea of this passage is that:

    A. prefabricated buildings are more international than those built on site.
    B. countries should work together more often in construction projects.
    C. the HSBC building was an international project.
    D. the HSBC building is well-known only because many countries were involved in its construction.

14. Many students solicit the advice of their school's academic guidance counselor to receive information about the admissions criteria of various colleges, as well as to seek help in registering for college admissions tests, such as the American College Test (ACT) or the Scholastic Aptitude Test (SAT). On the other hand, students without the drive to attend college upon graduation may choose to partake in various vocational courses offered through their local technical institute or academy.

    The Scholastic Aptitude Test:

    A. is taken in conjunction with the American College Test.
    B. is obligatory for students with vocational orientations.
    C. is administered by an academic guidance counselor.
    D. is an alternative to the American College Test.

15. In December 406 A.D. in what is now called Germany, fifteen thousand warriors crossed the frozen Rhine River and traveled into the Roman Empire of Gaul. A new historical epoch would soon be established in this former Roman Empire. Even though this period has diminished in historical significance in comparison to more recent events, the demise of the Roman Empire was certainly unprecedented in the fifth century. The six subsequent centuries that followed the collapse of the Roman Empire formed what we now call the Middle Ages.

    According to the passage, the Roman Empire of Gaul:

    A. was established during the Middle Ages.
    B. is now referred to as Germany.
    C. gradually collapsed throughout the Middle Ages.
    D. fell into ruin from 406 to 499 AD.

16. Many people consider ownership of an automobile to be an indispensable necessity for their day-to-day activities, but they simply cannot afford to patronize the expensive dealerships. Certain automotive manufacturers have found an innovative and ingenious solution to this dilemma: the compact car. Most consumers, even those earning a pittance, can afford these compact models.

    The new lines of compact cars:

    A. have created a dilemma for car buyers.
    B. are quite cheap, yet extravagant.
    C. can be purchased by consumers with low incomes.
    D. are sold only by elite dealerships.

17. The study of philosophy usually deals with two key problem areas: human choice and human thought. A consideration of both of these problem areas includes scientific and artistic viewpoints on the nature of human life. The first problem area, human choice, asks whether human beings can really make decisions that can change their futures. Conversely, it also investigates to what extent the individual's future is fixed and pre-determined by cosmic forces outside the control of human beings. In the second problem area, human thought, epistemology is considered. Epistemology means the study of knowledge; it should not be confused with ontology, the study of being or existence.

    The primary purpose of the passage is:

    A. to compare two different theories about an academic discipline.
    B. to explain key aspects of a particular area of study.
    C. to contrast scientific and artistic views on a particular topic.
    D. to investigate two troublesome aspects of human behavior.

18. Witnesses testify during a trial in court, giving testimony to implicate or exonerate the accused. The jury may find the accused innocent of the crime, whereupon he or she will be acquitted and released. On the other hand, the jury might find the accused guilty of the crime. The accused is then formally convicted of the crime, sentenced to the appropriate number of years for the violation, and imprisoned.

    Which of the following statements is false according to the passage?

    A. Once acquitted, the accused will be imprisoned.
    B. If found innocent, the accused is freed.
    C. The accused will be sentenced after being convicted of the crime.
    D. Witnesses may support or contradict the suspect's alibi.

19. In 1859, some of Abraham Lincoln's associates began to put forward the idea that he should run for President of the United States, a notion that he discounted in his usual self-deprecating manner. Nevertheless, as time passed, Lincoln began to write influential Republican Party leaders for their support. By 1860, Lincoln had garnered more public support, after having delivered public lectures and political speeches in various states. Despite being the underdog, Lincoln won 354 of the 466 total nominations at the Republican National Convention, and later, in November, 1860, the populace elected Lincoln as President of the United States.

    This passage is mainly about:

    A. the personal characteristics of Abraham Lincoln.
    B. the results of the 1860 election.
    C. how Lincoln ran for and won the United States Presidency.
    D. how to be successful as a politician.

20. If you want to be a serious television journalist, you may want to study journalism or broadcasting at college since some television networks consider academic training to be a very important prerequisite to obtaining these types of jobs. Of course, a whole host of traits will also come into play. For instance, having a speaking voice that is easy to understand is helpful. Above all, you should be quick-thinking and ready to respond logically to any challenge.

    For jobs in journalism, how should a person speak?

    A. loudly
    B. quickly
    C. clearly
    D. logically

Language Usage: This section of the test assesses your knowledge of English grammar. For the first part of this section, you must choose the word or phrase that makes a grammatically correct sentence. For the second part of this section, you will see two sentences. You must then choose a grammatically correct answer from the answer choices that has the same meaning as the two sentences provided.

21. _____ Rachel only once since she started college.
    A. I have seen   C. Did I see
    B. Have I seen   D. I saw

22. I finally _____ to buy this new car after I had looked at several models.
    A. to decide   C. decided
    B. deciding   D. had decided

23. All of the suspects denied _____ the car.
    A. stealing   C. to steal
    B. to stealing   D. to have stolen

24. My mother is very ill, so is _____ the hospital.
    A. in   C. within
    B. at   D. by

25. Iced tea is one of life's _____ pleasures.
    A. greater   C. most great
    B. greatest   D. the greatest

26. That restaurant has dishes that aren't _____ anywhere else.
    A. to be served   C. serving
    B. served   D. to serve

27. Never _____ skiing, I can't really say whether I like it.
    A. having tried   C. had tried
    B. to have tried   D. to try

28. We arrived at a solution that can _____.
    A. be easy done   C. be easily done
    B. easy to be done   D. easily to be done

29. The doctor advised me to do something that I never would have thought _____.
    A. to be done   C. to do
    B. to doing   D. of doing

30. It was time John _____ the situation.
    A. accept   C. accepted
    B. accepts   D. was accepting

31. Terry told everyone my secret. In spite of that, we are still good friends.
    A. In spite of Terry told everyone my secret, we are still good friends.
    B. In spite of Terry telling everyone my secret, we are still good friends.
    C. Despite Terry told everyone my secret, we are still good friends.
    D. Despite of Terry telling everyone my secret, we are still good friends.

32. Our company is going out of business. We didn't have enough customers.
    A. Because we didn't have enough customers, our company is going out of business.
    B. Because not enough customers, our company is going out of business.
    C. Due to not enough of customers, our company is going out of business.
    D. Resulting not having enough customers, our company is going out of business.

33. That device has one purpose. It is a machine that transmits documents.
    A. The purpose of that machine is transmission of documents.
    B. The purpose of that machine is for transmitting documents.
    C. The purpose of that machine is to transmit documents.
    D. The purpose of that machine is transmission documents.

34. I could not buy that new car. I did not have enough money.
    A. I would buy that new car if I had had enough money.
    B. I will buy that new car if I have enough money.
    C. I did not buy that new car without enough money.
    D. I would have bought that new car if I had had enough money.

35. I studied hard for my test. I was really disappointed when I did not pass it.
    A. I studied hard for my test, I was really disappointed when I did not pass it.
    B. Studying hard for my test, I was really disappointed when I did not pass it.
    C. Studied hard for my test, I was really disappointed when I did not pass it.
    D. Having studied hard for my test, I was really disappointed when I did not pass it.

36. I saw your boyfriend last night. He was in the park with his friends.
    A. With his friends, I saw in the park your boyfriend last night.
    B. I saw in the park your boyfriend last night with his friends.
    C. I saw your boyfriend in the park last night with his friends.
    D. I saw in the park with his friends your boyfriend last night.

37. The weather might improve soon. That would be better for everyone.
    A. An improvement in the weather. That would be better for everyone.
    B. An improvement in the weather, that would be better for everyone.
    C. An improvement in the weather would be better for everyone.
    D. An improvement in the weather, would be better for everyone.

38. The flight finally took off. It was delayed two hours.
    A. After delay of two hours, the flight finally took off.
    B. After delaying for two hours, the flight finally took off.
    C. After two hours delayed, the flight finally took off.
    D. After being delayed for two hours, the flight finally took off.

39. This neighborhood is so noisy. The people living here really do not like it.
    A. This neighborhood is so noisy that the people living here really do not like it.
    B. This neighborhood is so noisy, that people living here really do not like it.
    C. This neighborhood is so noisy, which the people living here really do not like it.
    D. This neighborhood is so noisy, the people living here really do not like it.

40. He got the promotion at work. His ability to work hard was the reason for it.
    A. His ability to work hard resulted in him to get the promotion at work.
    B. His ability to work hard resulted in him getting the promotion at work.
    C. His ability to work hard resulting in him to get the promotion at work.
    D. His ability to work hard resulting in him getting the promotion at work.

Sentence Meaning: This section tests your knowledge of English vocabulary. For the first part of this section, you must choose the correct word to fill in the gap in the sentence provided. For the second part of this section, you will read sentences that contain idioms. You must then choose the answer that best explains the idiom provided.

41. Ali is at home recovering _____ the flu.
    A. with
    B. for
    C. to
    D. from

42. The police solved the crime when the leader turned _____ the other criminals.
    A. down
    B. away
    C. off
    D. against

43. The child was _____ on his chewing gum.
    A. inhaling
    B. exhaling
    C. gnawing
    D. respiring

44. The situation was _____ with stress and tension.
    A. fraught
    B. blue
    C. manifest
    D. clandestine

45. The forest fire was _____ by a carelessly discarded cigarette.
    A. ignited
    B. burned
    C. helped
    D. forged

46. This painting _____ a battle in the Far East.
    A. looks
    B. depicts
    C. demonstrates
    D. views

47. Soon Li's proposal has many _____ , although it has positive points as well.
    A. benefits
    B. aspirations
    C. shortcomings
    D. advantages

48. The mother is often awarded _____ of the children in divorce proceedings.
    A. holding
    B. custody
    C. holdings
    D. custodies

49. After hours without food or water, the children began to _____ .
    A. procrastinate
    B. grumble
    C. stifle
    D. reproach

50. You've gotten a little _____ lately. Maybe you should go on a diet.
    A. plump
    B. shriveled
    C. thin
    D. nourished

51. Let's chip in to buy Yoko a birthday present.

    What are they going to do?
    A. Contribute money together for a present for Yoko.
    B. Buy individual presents for Yoko.
    C. Give Yoko money.
    D. Play a joke on Yoko.

52. After a year overseas, Bill longed to see his family back home.

    The speaker means that Bill:
    A. wants to see his family sooner or later.
    B. is far away from home.
    C. is eager to see his family.
    D. can wait to see his family.

53. We faced many stumbling blocks.

    What did they experience?
    A. expedients
    B. impediments
    C. advantages
    D. benefits

54. I just can't figure out the last exercise.

    The speaker means that:
    A. the exercise is difficult.
    B. he cannot solve the exercise.
    C. he does not have time to do the exercise.
    D. he does not want to do the exercise.

55. Juan got away with cheating.

   What happened to Juan?
   A. He was punished.
   B. He left the school.
   C. He was not caught.
   D. He failed the exam.

56. The last few months have taken their toll on him.

   The speaker means that:
   A. He has been badly affected by the past few months.
   B. The past few months have been expensive.
   C. He has had very poor health the past few months.
   D. He has lost the things that are most important to him.

57. I have decided to stick out college.

   The speaker will:
   A. return to college after a break.
   B. graduate from college.
   C. continue going to college.
   D. tell the teachers at college her opinions.

58. Can you keep a lid on it?

   The speaker is asking whether:
   A. you are listening.
   B. you can keep a secret.
   C. you want some food.
   D. you are relaxed.

59. Can you dig something up?

   The speaker is asking whether you:
   A. can leave something.
   B. can borrow something.
   C. can find something.
   D. can overlook something.

60. They covered it up.

   What did they do?
   A. cover something.
   B. reveal something.
   C. hide something.
   D. broke down something.

ACCUPLACER ESL LOEP – PRACTICE TEST 3

Reading Skills: For this section, you will read short passages and answer questions about them. Some questions will be about information which you can find directly in the passage. For other questions, you must make inferences from what you have read.

1. The National Transportation Safety Board, also known as the NTSB, was established on April 1, 1967. The NTSB was an independent body, but initially received financial and administrative support from the Department of Transportation (DoT). Under the Independent Safety Board Act of 1975, however, this organizational relationship was ultimately severed.

    What happened in 1975?

    A. The NTSB strengthened its relationship with the DoT.
    B. The NTSB ceased being affiliated with the DoT.
    C. The NTSB gained more financial support.
    D. The NTSB gained more administrative support.

2. While American Major League Baseball consisted of only a handful of teams when the National League was founded in 1876, baseball has grown in popularity by leaps and bounds over the years, resulting in increased ticket sales for games and bolstering the profits of its investors. The increased demand from the public, in turn, precipitated the formation of a new division, known as the American League, in 1901. Additionally, new teams are formed from time to time in accordance with regional demand, such as the Colorado Rockies in Denver, Colorado, and the Rays in Tampa Bay, Florida.

    The main purpose of the passage is:

    A. to give examples of two popular American baseball teams.
    B. to provide specific information about the process of forming new baseball teams.
    C. to trace historical developments relating to the popularity of baseball.
    D. to criticize Americans who depend on baseball for entertainment.

3. Deciduous trees lose their leaves every fall, at about the same time that flocks of wild birds migrate south for the winter. Evergreen trees, on the other hand, are not deciduous and remain green year-round. Trees such as the spruce, cedar, and pine have become popular for decorative purposes during the December holiday season, making this month an especially hectic time of year for farmers in this business.

    The passage describes:

    A. the production of deciduous trees for the holiday season.
    B. the harvest of fruit from evergreen trees.
    C. both seasonal and evergreen trees.
    D. certain species of birds.

4. A group of English separatists known as the Pilgrims left England to live in Amsterdam in 1608. After spending a few years in their new city, however, many members of the group felt that they did not have enough independence. So, in 1617, the pilgrims decided to leave Amsterdam to immigrate to America. Many of these separatists were poor farmers who did not have much education or social status. In addition, the group had many financial problems that prevented them from beginning their journey.

   What prevented the Pilgrims from beginning their journey to America?

   A. lack of education
   B. lack of social status
   C. lack of financing
   D. lack of independence

5. The use of computers in the stock market helps to control national and international finance. Although these controls were originally designed in order to create long-term monetary stability and protect shareholders from catastrophic losses, the high level of automation now involved in buying and selling shares means that computer-to-computer trading could result in a downturn in the stock market. Such a slump in the market, if not properly regulated, could bring about a computer-led stock market crash. For this reason, regulations have been put in place by NASDAQ, AMEX, and FTSE.

   From this passage, one could infer that:

   A. regulations on computer-to-computer trading are considered to be a financial necessity.
   B. there are negative public views about regulations on computer-to-computer trading.
   C. NASDAQ, AMEX, and FTSE were initially opposed to establishing regulations on computer-to-computer trading.
   D. the role of computers in international markets has not been modified over time.

6. When any big meal is finished, there are likely to be left-overs. These can be put in the refrigerator to eat over the next few days. Unfortunately, the kitchen may be left untidy with stacks of dirty dishes, and the tablecloth is likely to be stained.

   A big meal culminates in:

   A. piles of unclean dishes
   B. immaculate tablecloths
   C. impeccable kitchens
   D. all of the above

7. Airline travel is generally considered to be an extremely safe mode of transportation. In fact, statistics reveal that far fewer individuals are killed each year in airline accidents than in crashes involving automobiles. In spite of this safety record, airlines deploy ever-increasingly strict standards governing the investigation of aircraft crashes. Information gleaned from the investigation of aircraft crashes is utilized in order to prevent such tragedies from occurring again in the future.

The main purpose of this passage is:

A. to contrast automotive travel with airline travel.
B. to compare statistics on deaths related to transportation accidents.
C. to explain the reasons for the investigation of aircraft crashes.
D. to justify government spending on aircraft accident investigations.

8. Senior citizens can fall prey to various infirmities later in life, but elderly patients are sometimes discharged from the hospital prematurely to recuperate at home simply because they are not adequately insured. Some have argued that if the health care system cannot provide care for those who need it most, namely the feeble and frail, it is of no real use whatsoever.

According to the passage, senior citizens:

A. usually stay at the hospital too long.
B. are usually in poor health.
C. are admitted to the hospital too early.
D. are sometimes forced to convalesce at home.

9. In 1749, British surveyors spotted a high peak in the distant range of the Himalayas. More than one hundred years later, in 1852, another survey was completed, which confirmed that this peak was the highest mountain in the world. Later named Mount Everest, this peak was considered to be the world's highest mountain until 1986. At that time, George Wallerstein from the University of Washington posited that another Himalayan mountain, named K-2, was higher than Everest. It took an expedition of Italian scientists, who used a surfeit of technological devices, to disprove Wallerstein's claim.

According to the passage, which one of the following statements is correct?

A. Since 1749, Mount Everest has universally been considered to be the tallest mountain in the world.
B. Wallerstein fell into disrepute in the academic community after his claims were disproved.
C. The Italian team confirmed that Everest was, in fact, the tallest mountain in the world.
D. In spite of a lack of technologically-advanced equipment, Italian scientists were able to refute Wallerstein's hypothesis.

10. Clones have been used for centuries in the field of horticulture. For instance, florists have traditionally made clones of geraniums and other plants by taking cuttings and re-planting them in fresh soil. Despite the predictability of cloning in the realm of plants and flowers, cloning in other areas has arguably taken on sinister undertones, thanks to the rapid development of science and technology. Some fear the ethical ramifications that will inevitably occur if cloning is extended to the human species.

    We can conclude from the information in this passage that:

    A. the subject of cloning has become somewhat controversial.
    B. cloning has fallen out of favor with horticulturalists.
    C. in spite of certain misgivings, many people support human cloning.
    D. technological advances have impeded the use of cloning.

11. Some people believe that the profession of teaching is replete with difficulties these days. Of course, state high schools receive money from the government for their support, and the purchase of resources such as books, equipment, and facilities depends on this financial assistance. If the national or state economy experiences a downturn, this can have a negative effect on the funding available to help schools. Because of these and other demands, some teachers have changed careers after deciding that the demands of the educational system and state bureaucracy have made their work too stressful.

    Why have some teachers changed careers?

    A. because they have become bored with teaching
    B. because they have found their work too trying
    C. because they failed to receive personal financial assistance
    D. because of a boom in the economy

12. In order to ignite a campfire, one must search for fallen debris, such as twigs, branches, and hollow tree trunks, in the woods. The fire is ignited by striking two pieces of flint together. When the first flicker appears, it is necessary to watch and fuel the fire. For the purpose of cooking, pots and kettles may be hung over the fire.

    Which of the following statements about campfires is true?

    A. It is prepared from forged materials.
    B. It must be closely monitored to prevent it from being extinguished.
    C. Once it is ignited, will continue to burn until morning.
    D. It usually burns out before a meal can be prepared.

13. Owing to the powerful and destructive nature of tornadoes, there are a number of myths and misconceptions surrounding them. For instance, many people mistakenly believe that tornadoes never occur over rivers, lakes, and oceans; yet, waterspouts, tornadoes that form over bodies of water, often move onshore and cause extensive damage to coastal areas. In addition, tornadoes can accompany hurricanes and tropical storms as they move to land. Another common myth about tornadoes is that damage to structures like houses and office buildings can be avoided if windows are opened prior to the impact of the storm.

    What can be inferred about the public's knowledge of tornadoes?

    A. A large number of people know how to avoid tornado damage.
    B. Most people appreciate the risk of death associated with tornadoes.
    C. Some members of the public know how to regulate the pressure inside buildings.
    D. Many people are not fully aware of certain key information about tornadoes.

14. Born in France in 1896, Jean Piaget was one of the most influential thinkers in the area of child development in the twentieth century. Piaget posited that children go through a stage of assimilation as they grow to maturity. Assimilation refers to the process of transforming one's innate cognitive schemes for use in different situations. For instance, schemes used in infant breast feeding and bottle feeding are examples of assimilation because the child utilizes his or her innate capacity for sucking to complete both tasks.

    Why does the writer mention bottle feeding in the above paragraph?

    A. to identify one of the important features of assimilation.
    B. to exemplify the assimilation process.
    C. to describe the importance of assimilation.
    D. to explain difficulties children face during assimilation.

15. Inherent social and cultural biases pervaded the manner in which archeological findings were investigated during the early nineteenth century because little attention was paid to the roles that wealth, status, and nationality played in the recovery and interpretation of the artifacts. However, in the 1860's Charles Darwin established the theory that human beings are the ultimate product of a long biological evolutionary process. Darwinian theory infiltrated the discipline of archeology and heavily influenced the manner in which archeological artifacts were recovered and analyzed. As a result of Darwinism, there was a surge in artifacts excavated from African and Asian localities by the late 1900's.

    Based on the information above, what can be inferred about the early 1900's?

    A. There were few archeological findings from Africa and Asia.
    B. Darwinian theory had little effect on archeology.
    C. All archeological findings were culturally biased in the early 1900's.
    D. Charles Darwin was responsible for the recovery of many artifacts.

16. External forces and market conditions can have a huge impact on personal financial situations. Consumables such as groceries often go up in price a few pennies between shopping trips. When the prices of goods jump up by a slightly larger amount, there can be enormous consequences in the value of commodities in the worldwide market. I note the price of petroleum products as it relates to world financial affairs as a case in point.

    The writer uses the price of petroleum products as an example mainly to:

    A. imply that the demand for petroleum products is responsible for many problems with world affairs.
    B. illustrate the connection between market conditions and prices.
    C. suggest that an excessive demand for petroleum products leads to increases in petroleum product prices.
    D. discuss commodities in the worldwide market.

17. The tradition of music in the western world originated in the genre of chanting. Chant, a monophonic form of music, was the dominant mode of music for hundreds of years prior to the thirteenth century. The word "monophonic" is Greek in origin, and it means "one sound." Accordingly, monophonic music consists of only one sound or voice that combines various notes in a series.

    The main idea of this passage is to describe:

    A. the origins of music in the western world.
    B. the history of music during two previous centuries.
    C. the semantics of a particular Greek word.
    D. the variety of symphonic forms.

18. Various health risks are posed by processed or convenience food. Packaged food often contains chemicals, such as additives to enhance the color of the food or preservatives that give the food a longer life. Food additives are detrimental to health for a number of reasons. First of all, they are not natural and may perhaps be linked to disease in the long term. In addition, they may block the body's ability to absorb energy and nutrients from food, such as essential vitamins and minerals that are required for healthy bodily function.

    How does the passage support its claim about food additives?

    A. by explaining their purpose
    B. by giving reasons for their dangers
    C. by discussing specific medical case studies
    D. by linking them to preservatives

19. The Olympic Games, which have a long and rich history, were originally part of a local festival. Nowadays, the opening ceremony of the games is held in a stadium in a major city. After the Parade of Nations, in which the athletes march around the stadium with flags that represent their host countries, the athletes take the Olympic Oath. The games, which are said to promote friendship and understanding among nations, then officially begin.

    What happens during the Parade of Nations?

    A. The athletes take the Olympic Oath.
    B. The athletes compete in their first event.
    C. The athletes march around the stadium.
    D. The athletes participate in a local festival.

20. Running for the office of the President of the United States is exceptionally arduous and should not be undertaken by the faint-hearted. The candidates must first compete in the local primary elections. During the primary campaign, the candidate endeavors to gain the votes of his or her constituents. Any new candidates are the opponents to the incumbent, the President currently in office who is running for re-election. During this time, the candidates strive to develop rapport between themselves and the public.

    When attempting to be elected as President, candidates:

    A. try not to create animosity with the public.
    B. should be retiring and timid.
    C. must be servile.
    D. attempt to alienate voters during the primary campaign.

Language Usage: This section of the test assesses your knowledge of English grammar. For the first part of this section, you must choose the word or phrase that makes a grammatically correct sentence. For the second part of this section, you will see two sentences. You must then choose a grammatically correct answer from the answer choices that has the same meaning as the two sentences provided.

21. The store was destroyed as a result of the fire, and they _____ re-build everything.
    A. will have had   C. will have to
    B. will have had to   D. have had

22. _____ painting, Anna can also draw.
    A. apart   C. instead
    B. except   D. besides

23. The new supermarket _____ next week.
    A. be opening   C. is being opening
    B. will opening   D. is having its opening

24. I'll _____ you at the corner of Fifth and Main.
    A. waiting
    B. be waiting
    C. be waiting for
    D. waiting for

25. Next time we'll have to _____ sign her name more clearly.
    A. made her
    B. make her
    C. made her to
    D. make her to

26. Carlos is _____ his three brothers.
    A. taller of
    B. taller than
    C. the tallest
    D. tallest of

27. I really regret _____ harder to increase my savings.
    A. not having tried
    B. not to have tried
    C. not to try
    D. not to trying

28. Wei Li _____ me to repeat something four times yesterday.
    A. had asked
    B. has been asking
    C. asked
    D. had been asking

29. Just after we _____ , he left.
    A. had arrived
    B. were arriving
    C. have arrived
    D. were arrived

30. My grandma is coming to visit me _____ the beginning of the month.
    A. in
    B. on
    C. at
    D within

31. I heard Pablo speaking. He was speaking very loudly.
    A. He was speaking so loudly, and I heard Pablo.
    B. Since speaking so loudly, I heard Pablo.
    C. I heard Pablo since he was speaking so loudly.
    D. I heard Pablo since speaking so loudly.

32. Anabel lost her job. Of course, she is very upset about it.
    A. Need less to say, Anabel is very upset about losing her job.
    B. Needless to say, Anabel is very upset about losing her job.
    C. Need less to say, Anabel is very upset about lost her job.
    D. Needless to say, Anabel is very upset about lost her job.

33. I do not know the directions to Chicago very well. I think it is on Route 66.
    A. I do not know the directions to Chicago very well, I think it is on Route 66.
    B. Not knowing the directions to Chicago very well, I think it is on Route 66.
    C. I do not know the directions to Chicago very well, but I think it is on Route 66.
    D. I do not know the directions to Chicago very well, however I think it is on Route 66.

34. He likes coffee. He drinks his coffee black.
    A. He likes drinking coffee when black.
    B. He likes to drink his coffee when black.
    C. He likes to drinking his coffee black.
    D. He likes drinking his coffee black.

35. Our business was making a good income. We have just sold it.
    A. We have just sold our business, which was making a good income.
    B. We have just sold our business, that was making a good income.
    C. Making a good income, we have just sold our business.
    D. We have just sold our business, making a good income.

36. Pilar wants to go shopping when she gets here. Let's go with her.
    A. Let's go with Pilar shopping when she gets here.
    B. Let's go shopping with Pilar when she gets here.
    C. Let's go to shop with Pilar when she gets here.
    D. When Pilar gets here, let's go to shop.

37. Abdul is a good student. He gets better grades than all of the other students in his class.
    A. Abdul gets better grades of all of the students in his class.
    B. Abdul gets the better grades than all of the students in his class.
    C. Abdul gets the best grades of all of the students in his class.
    D. Abdul gets the best grades than all of the students in his class.

38. Tomas enjoys golfing. He also likes to swim.
    A. Tomas enjoys golfing and to swim.
    B. Tomas enjoys golfing and swimming.
    C. Tomas enjoys to go golfing and swim.
    D. Tomas enjoys to golf and swimming.

39. He didn't pay the money back to you. I wouldn't trust him anymore.
    A. Because he didn't pay the money back to you, I wouldn't trust him anymore.
    B. Because of he didn't pay the money back to you, I wouldn't trust him anymore.
    C. He didn't pay the money back to you, therefore I wouldn't trust him anymore.
    D. He didn't pay the money back to you, I wouldn't trust him anymore.

40. Nikos has strong opinions. Besides that, I like him.
    A. Besides having strong opinions, I like Nikos.
    B. Besides strong opinions, I like Nikos.
    C. Apart from his strong opinions, I like Nikos.
    D. Apart from strong opinions, I like Nikos.

Sentence Meaning: This section tests your knowledge of English vocabulary. For the first part of this section, you must choose the correct word to fill in the gap in the sentence provided. For the second part of this section, you will read sentences that contain idioms. You must then choose the answer that best explains the idiom provided.

41. Only a small _____ of the class passed the examination.
    A. ratio
    B. ration
    C. number
    D. fraction

42. He _____ his desk drawers, looking for his wallet.
    A. searched
    B. saw
    C. viewed
    D. watched

43. The old building fell _____ with the help of explosives.
    A. upon
    B. down
    C. under
    D. below

44. Hassan is quite _____ at using the computer.
    A. scrambled
    B. skilled
    C. scanty
    D. scared

45. The department store was _____ with customers when it reduced its prices 50%.
    A. inundated
    B. hushed
    C. profligate
    D. abashed

46. What you said really _____ me. Please tell me more.
    A. relegates
    B. lingers
    C. intrigues
    D. subjugates

47. Prices _____ during times of scarcity.
    A. recuperate
    B. scorch
    C. skyrocket
    D. splinter

48. The situation is _____ , and there is little hope for improvement.
    A. foremost
    B. bleak
    C. dispensable
    D. comprehensive

49. Her aunt is a very _____ woman and has many unusual habits.
    A. infirm
    B. appliance
    C. insurmountable
    D. unconventional

50. She has proved to be a _____-weather friend. She didn't help me at the time I needed it most.
    A. hard
    B. fair
    C. foul
    D. poor

51. I can put up with her.

    The speaker means that she:
    A. can tolerate her.
    B. likes her.
    C. can't stand her.
    D. is good friends with her.

52. Don't throw in the towel!

    The speaker is telling someone to:
    A. to be realistic.
    B. to be serious.
    C. not to give up.
    D. not to accept the circumstances.

53. Smoking is frowned upon.

    In other words, smoking:
    A. is not permitted.
    B. is dangerous.
    C. makes people unhappy.
    D. is being discouraged.

54. Her story doesn't hold water.

    The speaker means that her story:
    A. is fascinating.
    B. is untrue.
    C. is unimportant.
    D. means nothing.

55. Marisa hit the nail on the head.

    What did Marisa do?
    A. She said something appropriate.
    B. She built something new.
    C. She made people angry.
    D. She started a discussion.

56. That would be like looking for a needle in a haystack.

    The speaker means that it would be:
    A. urgent
    B. difficult
    C. impossible
    D. worth the time

57. Julio was just beating around the bush.

 What was Julio doing?
 A. being evasive
 B. causing trouble
 C. working in the garden
 D. trying to find something

58. I could go for that!

 The speaker:
 A. wants to travel.
 B. is in the mood for something.
 C. is disagreeing with someone.
 D. is telling someone to leave.

59. Don't take it out on me!

 The speaker is telling someone not to:
 A. speak to them.
 B. go out with them.
 C. punish them for someone else's mistake.
 D. bring them something.

60. This club accepts members from all walks of life.

 The club:
 A. is for walking expeditions.
 B. is very welcoming.
 C. has various activities.
 D. has too many members.

ANSWERS – TEST 1

1. C
2. D
3. B
4. C
5. A
6. D
7. C
8. C
9. D
10. D
11. A
12. B
13. C
14. D
15. B
16. A
17. B
18. D
19. A
20. C
21. A
22. B
23. A
24. A
25. C
26. D
27. B
28. C
29. B
30. A

31. C
32. B
33. D
34. C
35. D
36. A
37. A
38. B
39. B
40. B
41. A
42. C
43. B
44. A
45. D
46. D
47. D
48. A
49. B
50. B
51. A
52. C
53. D
54. D
55. A
56. A
57. B
58. C
59. B
60. A

© COPYRIGHT 1995, 2016 Academic Success Media. © COPYRIGHT 2020 Academic Success Group.
This material may not be copied or reproduced in any form.

ANSWERS – TEST 2

1. B
2. A
3. D
4. A
5. A
6. B
7. C
8. C
9. A
10. C
11. B
12. B
13. C
14. D
15. D
16. C
17. B
18. A
19. C
20. C
21. A
22. C
23. A
24. A
25. B
26. B
27. A
28. C
29. D
30. C
31. B
32. A
33. C
34. D
35. D
36. C
37. C
38. D
39. A
40. B
41. D
42. D
43. C
44. A
45. A
46. B
47. C
48. B
49. B
50. A
51. A
52. C
53. B
54. B
55. C
56. A
57. C
58. B
59. C
60. C

ANSWERS – TEST 3

1. B
2. C
3. C
4. C
5. A
6. A
7. C
8. D
9. C
10. A
11. B
12. B
13. D
14. B
15. A
16. B
17. A
18. B
19. C
20. A
21. C
22. D
23. D
24. C
25. B
26. B
27. A
28. C
29. A
30. C

31. C
32. B
33. C
34. D
35. A
36. B
37. C
38. B
39. A
40. C
41. D
42. A
43. B
44. B
45. A
46. C
47. C
48. B
49. D
50. B
51. A
52. C
53. D
54. B
55. A
56. C
57. A
58. B
59. C
60. B

ACCUPLACER ESL LOEP STUDY GUIDE

The following sections of the study guide give information about and examples of the grammar and idioms most commonly tested on the Accuplacer ESL LOEP test.

Part 1 - Grammar Guide

Verb tense and form:

VERB TENSES:

There are six *basic* verb tenses in English.

> Present: I walk.
>
> Past: I walked.
>
> Future: I will walk.
>
> Present Perfect: I have walked.
>
> Past Perfect: I had walked.
>
> Future Perfect: I will have walked.

There are also *continuous* verbs forms, which are not illustrated in the above examples.

There are many *irregular* verb forms in English. An irregular verb is one that does not take -ed to form the simple past tenses. Look at these examples:

> Regular verb - simple present: I work in a factory.
>
> Regular verb - simple past: I worked in a factory when I was younger.
>
> Irregular verb - simple present: I eat chocolate quite often.
>
> Irregular verb - simple past: I ate chocolate yesterday afternoon.

SUBJECT VERB AGREEMENT:

Singular grammatical subject:

> The child in boy scouts knows how to light a fire.

child = singular subject; knows = verb; ["scouts" is part of a prepositional phrase]

Plural grammatical subject:

> Many residents of the local community are on good terms with one another.

Residents = plural subject; are = verb; ["community" is part of a prepositional phrase]

Vern tense and form are reviewed further on page 114.

ACTIVE AND PASSIVE VERB FORMS:

Active: First, the teacher gave the students a card showing a role-play scenario.

Passive: First, the students *were given* a card showing a role-play scenario *by the teacher.*

Comparatives and superlatives:

Use the comparative form when comparing two things.

The comparative form consists of the adjective plus –er when the adjective has two syllables or less: pretty → prettier

When the adjective has more than two syllables, the adjective should be preceded by the word "more" in order to form the comparative:

> beautiful → more beautiful

Examples:

> Tom is taller than his brother.
>
> Tom is more intelligent than his brother.

If you are comparing more than two things, you must use the superlative form.

As a general rule, the superlative form consists of the adjective plus –est when the adjective has two syllables or less:

> pretty → prettiest

To form the superlative for adjectives that have more than two syllables, the adjective should be preceded by the word "most":

> beautiful → most beautiful

Examples:

>Tom is the tallest boy in his class.
>
>Tom is the most intelligent boy in his class.

Conditional sentences:

Conditional sentences often begin with the word "if." Conditional sentences can also begin with phrases such as "provided that" or "on condition that."

Conditional sentences may address hypothetical or imaginary situations.

When discussing hypothetical situations, the simple present tense is used in the *if* clause, and the auxiliary verb *will* is used in the main part of the sentence.

Example:

>If I get good grades, I will get a better scholarship.

Conditional sentences may express generalizations. In other words, conditional sentences can be used to talk about general truths or things that always happen under certain conditions.

Example:

>If I go out alone after dark, I try to be alert and careful.

For this type of conditional, the simple present tense (go) is used in the *if* clause, and the simple present (try) is also used in the main part of the sentence.

Conditional sentences may involve the use of the subjunctive verb form. This means that you need to use "were" instead of "was" when describing hypothetical situations about yourself. Therefore, the verb "were" is used in the part of the sentence that describes the condition, and the verb "would" is used in the part of the sentence that describes the imaginary outcome.

Examples:

>CORRECT – If I were a millionaire, I would quit my job.
>
>INCORRECT – If I was a millionaire, I would quit my job.

The two parts of a conditional sentence must be separated by a comma when the *if* clause is placed before the main clause of the sentence.

Gerunds and infinitives:

A gerund is a verbal noun which ends in "ing," while the infinitive consists of "to" and the base form of the verb.

Some verbs always take an infinitive (to + verb) and some always take a gerund (the -ing form). However, some will take either.

Look at the following examples:

> Other buyers may contemplate *purchasing* more expensive cars.
>
> Many people cannot afford *to patronize* expensive stores.

INFINITIVE:

> CORRECT – Sarah decided to go out.
>
> INCORRECT – Sarah decided going out.

GERUND:

> CORRECT – Sarah suggested going out.
>
> INCORRECT – Sarah suggested to go out.

Here are some more examples:

> He agreed to pay half the cost.
>
> He recommended paying half the cost.
>
> She refused to wait.
>
> I practice playing the piano.
>
> The man had chosen not to buy a ticket.
>
> She admitted not buying a ticket.

So, as you can see, some verbs take gerunds and some take infinitives.

You should study the following lists in order to remember which verbs take the infinitive form and which verbs take the gerund form.

<u>These verbs and phrases take the infinitive:</u>

agree

aim

appear

arrange

ask

attempt

be just about (ready)

beg

can't afford

can't wait

choose

claim

decide

demand

expect

fail

guarantee

happen

hesitate

hope

it's time

learn

long

manage

mean

neglect

offer

omit

pay

plan

prepare

pretend

promise

prove

refuse

seem

swear

tend

there's no reason

threaten

turn out

want

wish

These verbs and phrases take the gerund:

admit

appreciate

avoid

be in the habit of

be tired of

can't help

can't stand

confess

consider

contemplate

delay

deny

detest

dislike

don't mind

enjoy

escape

excuse

finish

give up

have trouble

How about . . .?

imagine

involve

justify

keep

keep on

mention

miss

not be worth

postpone

practice

put off

quit

recommend

resent

resist

risk

save

suggest

thinking about

thought of

tolerate

These verbs can take either the infinitive or the gerund: start, continue, intend, like, and hate.

For example, both of these sentences are correct:

    CORRECT: Andrew started to unpack his suitcase.

    CORRECT: Andrew started unpacking his suitcase.

Notice the difference between the following examples.

CORRECT: It's not worth writing the whole letter over again.

INCORRECT: It's not worth to write whole letter over again.

Important tip for the exam: Remember that when you are discussing hobbies or pastimes, you should use the -ing form.

Misplaced modifiers:

Modifiers are phrases that describe other parts of a sentence. The modifier should always be placed directly before or after the noun to which it relates.

Now look at these examples:

INCORRECT: Like Minnesota, it gets extremely cold in Wisconsin in the winter.

CORRECT: Like Minnesota, Wisconsin gets extremely cold in the winter.

The phrase "like Minnesota" is an adjectival phrase that modifies the noun "Wisconsin."

Therefore, "Wisconsin" must come directly after the comma.

Here are two more examples:

INCORRECT: While at the mall, a robbery was committed.

CORRECT: While at the mall, a gang of youths committed a robbery.

The adverbial phrase "while at the mall" modifies the noun phrase "a gang of youths."

So, this noun phrase needs to come after the adverbial phrase.

Restrictive and non-restrictive modifiers:

Restrictive modifiers are clauses or phrases that provide essential information in order to identify the subject of the sentence. Restrictive modifiers should not be preceded with a comma.

Example: My sister who lives in Indianapolis is a good swimmer.

In this case, the speaker has more than one sister, and she is identifying which sister she is talking about by giving the essential information "who lives in Indianapolis."

On the other hand, a non-restrictive modifier is a clause or phrase that provides extra information about a grammatical subject in a sentence. A non-restrictive modifier must be preceded by a comma.

Example: My sister, who lives in Indianapolis, is a good swimmer.

In this case, the speaker has only one sister. Therefore, the information about her sister's city of residence is not essential in order to identify which sister she is talking about.

So, the words "who lives in Indianapolis" form a non-restrictive modifier.

Negative inversion:

When a sentence begins with a negative phrase [no sooner, not only, never, never before etc.], the past perfect tense [had + past participle] must be used.

In addition, the auxiliary verb "had" must be inverted. In other words, the auxiliary verb "had" is placed in front of the grammatical subject of the sentence.

Placing the auxiliary verb in front of the grammatical subject in this way is known as negative inversion.

INCORRECT: Never in my life I have seen such a beautiful sight.

CORRECT: Never in my life have I seen such a beautiful sight.

Past participle phrases:

Past participle verb forms are often similar to the past simple tense form.

In other words, past participles end in –ed in cases of regular verbs.

For example, the past participle of the verb "fluster" is "flustered."

Remember to put the past participle phrase immediately before or after the noun it modifies.

Also remember to use commas before and after the past participle phrase.

CORRECT: Flustered, Eva failed her driving test.

INCORRECT: Flustered Eva failed her driving test.

Past participle phrases can also be longer than one word, as in the following example:

> CORRECT: Unperturbed by the day's events, Mark relaxed for the evening.

> INCORRECT: Unperturbed by the day's events Mark relaxed for the evening.

Past perfect tense:

The past perfect is often used to talk about an action that has just recently occurred. It can also be used when a sentence describes two actions in order to show that one action preceded the other.

In these types of sentences, the past perfect is used for the action which happened first. The simple past is used for the subsequent action.

Look at this example:

> After the group of southern states had consolidated, they called themselves the Confederate States of America.

In other words, the consolidation occurred first. After this, the states began to call themselves the new name.

The past perfect is often used with the words "just" and "after," and with the phrase "no sooner... than."

REMEMBER: The auxiliary verb must come before the word "just."

> Example: When we had just arrived, she decided to leave.

Punctuation and independent clauses:

An independent clause contains a grammatical subject and verb. It therefore can stand alone as its own sentence. It should begin with a capital letter and be preceded with a period.

> INCORRECT: I thought I would live in this city forever, then I lost my job.

> CORRECT: I thought I would live in this city forever. Then I lost my job.

"Then I lost my job" is a complete sentence. It has a grammatical subject [I] and a verb [lost]. So, an independent clause must be preceded by a period, and the new sentence must begin with a capital letter.

Alternatively, an appropriate conjunction can be used to join the independent clauses:

Example: I thought I would live in this city forever, and then I lost my job.

Punctuation and quotation marks:

Punctuation should be enclosed within the final quotation mark when giving dialogue.

> INCORRECT: "I can't believe you bought a new car", Sam remarked.

> CORRECT: "I can't believe you bought a new car," Sam remarked.

In the example below, the word "exclaimed" shows that the exclamation point is needed.

> INCORRECT: "I can't believe you bought a new car"! Sam exclaimed.

> CORRECT: "I can't believe you bought a new car!" Sam exclaimed.

Sentence linking words and phrases:

Sentence linking words and phrases are tested extensively on the Accuplacer ESL, especially on the language usage part of the test. When you are choosing your answer from the options provided, pay attention to sentence construction, as well as punctuation.

Sentence linking words and phrases fall into three categories.

TYPE 1 – SENTENCE LINKERS

Sentence linkers are usually used at the beginning of a sentence and are followed by a comma.

Sentence linker example:

> *However*, you should still study hard.

For emphasis, you can use sentence linkers in the middle of a sentence. If you use a sentence linker in the middle of a sentence, be sure that you put commas both before and after the sentence linker:

> You should, however, still study hard.

TYPE 2 – PHRASE LINKERS

Phrase linkers must be followed by a noun or noun phrase. Phrase linkers should not be followed by a clause.

Phrase linker example 1 – no comma:

> He passed the exam *because of* his hard work.

"His hard work" is a noun phrase. In other words, it does not contain a verb.

Remember that verbs are words that show action.

<u>Phrase linker example 2 – with comma:</u>

>*Because of* his hard work, he passed the exam.

When the sentence begins with the phrase linker, we classify the sentence as an inverted sentence.

Notice that you will need to place a comma between the two parts of the sentence when the sentence is inverted.

TYPE 3 – SUBORDINATORS

Subordinators must be followed by a clause. Subordinators should not be followed by a phrase.

The two clauses of a subordinated sentence are normally separated by a comma.

Remember that clauses must contain a grammatical subject and a verb.

<u>Subordinator examples:</u>

>*Although* he worked hard, he failed to make his business successful.

>He failed to make his business successful, *although* he worked hard.

Although is a subordinator. In the above example sentences, *he worked hard* is a clause. The verb is *worked* and the grammatical subject is *he*.

Now look at the groups of sentence linking words and phrases below. Note which ones are sentence linkers, which ones are phrase linkers, and which ones are subordinators.

<u>Sentence linkers for giving additional information</u>
further
furthermore
apart from this
what is more
in addition
additionally
in the same way
moreover

Sentence linkers for giving examples

for example

for instance

in this case

in particular

mainly

more precisely

namely

in brief

in short

Sentence linkers for stating the obvious

obviously

clearly

naturally

of course

surely

after all

Sentence linkers for giving generalizations

in general

on the whole

as a rule

for the most part

generally speaking

in most cases

Sentence linkers for stating causes and effects

thus

accordingly

hence

therefore

in that case

under those circumstances

as a result

for this reason

as a consequence

consequently

in effect

Sentence linkers for showing contrast

on the other hand

on the contrary

alternatively

rather

Phrase linker for showing contrast

in contrast to

Sentence linkers for showing similarity

similarly

in the same way

likewise

Phrase linker for showing similarity

just as

Sentence linkers for paraphrasing or restating

in other words

that is to say

that is

Subordinators

after

although

as

because

before

even though

if

since

so that

unless

until

when

where

while

who

whom

whose

whereas

not only . . . but also

<u>Sentence linkers for concession or unexpected results</u>

however

nevertheless

still

yet

meanwhile

<u>Phrase linkers for concession or unexpected results</u>

despite

in spite of

<u>Sentence linkers for giving conclusions</u>

finally

to conclude

lastly

in conclusion

to sum up

in summary

Part 2 - Grammar Practice

Grammar Exercise 1: Negative Adverbial Clauses

When a sentence begins with a negative adverb, the auxiliary verb is inverted. In other words, the auxiliary verb is placed in front of the grammatical subject of the sentence, instead of being in its usual position, which is next to the main verb. Therefore, an inverted sentence follows this pattern:

Negative adverb + auxiliary verb + grammatical subject + main verb

Look at this example and notice how it follows the pattern given above:

Not only do sports exist as a source of entertainment for the American public, but also as a lucrative business enterprise for those who provide financial backing.

Not only (negative adverb) + do (auxiliary verb) + sports (grammatical subject) + exist (main verb)

If this sentence were not inverted, it would look like this:

Sports exist not only as a source of entertainment for the American public, but also as a lucrative business enterprise for those who provide financial backing.

Notice that the word "do" is added when the sentence is inverted.

Here are some negative adverbs that are commonly encountered on the Accuplacer examination:

never	never before
not	only when
only once	seldom
rarely	hardly ever

These negative adverbs can be placed into five categories:

TYPE 1: If the original sentence contains an auxiliary verb, such as "would," "had," or "did" the auxiliary verb is inverted.

Example:
Original sentence: I had seen her only once before then.
Inverted sentence: Only once before then had I seen her.

TYPE 2: If the original sentence does not contain an auxiliary verb, the verb "do" is used in the inverted sentence.

Example:
Original sentences: Farah not only failed the driving test, she also had an accident.
Inverted sentence: Not only did Farah fail the driving test, she also had an accident.

TYPE 3: If the original sentence is in the negative (i.e., if it contains the words "not" or "never"), the negative word is placed at the beginning of the inverted sentence.

Examples:
Original sentence: Loli didn't tell a single person her secret.
Inverted sentence: Not a single person did Loli tell her secret.

Original sentence: I have never experienced anything like that before.
Inverted sentence: Never before have I experienced anything like that.

TYPE 4: If the original sentence contains the word "when," the inverted sentence begins "Only when." You may also need to add "do" to the second part of the inverted sentence.

Example:
Original sentence: Alberto remembered his co-worker's name when they had finished their conversation.
Inverted sentence: Only when they had finished their conversation did Alberto remember his co-worker's name.

TYPE 5: If the original sentence contains an adverb of frequency such as "often" or "not often," the inverted sentence can begin with "Seldom," "Rarely," or "Hardly ever."

Example:
Original sentence: Marcus doesn't go on vacation often.
Inverted sentence: Rarely does Marcus go on vacation.

Exercise: Write a new sentence as similar as possible in meaning to the sentence provided, using the negative adverbial phrases indicated below. It may be helpful to identify the type of sentence by looking at the examples above.

1)   Bread would not be available at the grocery store until noon.

        Not until . . .

2)   Frank realized he had forgotten to fill up his truck when it ran out of gas.

        Only when . . .

3)   I have never changed a flat tire in my life.

        Never before . . .

4)   I realized who he was when he took off his sunglasses.

        Only when . . .

5) I have never seen such an exciting football game in my life.
Never . . .

6) John didn't say a word during the entire drive home.
Not . . .

7) A teenager seldom flunks his driving test the first time.
Rarely . . .

8) Jane doesn't stay out past midnight very often.
Seldom . . .

9) I have seen the Grand Canyon only one time.
Only once . .

10) He rarely has time to see his parents since he has gone away to college.
Hardly ever . . .

Grammar Exercise 2: Past Perfect

The past perfect is often used to express an action which has just recently occurred. It can also be used to show that one action preceded another when a sentence describes two actions. In this situation, the past perfect is used for the action which happened first. The simple past is used for the subsequent action.

Look at this example:

> Their adversaries in the southern states, the Confederates, had consolidated and called themselves the Confederate States of America.

In other words, the consolidation occurred first. After this, the states began to call themselves the new name.

The past perfect is often used with the words "just" and "after," and with the phrase "no sooner. . . than. "

REMEMBER: The auxiliary verb must come before the word "just."

Example: When we had just arrived, she decided to leave.

NOTE: "No sooner" is a negative adverbial. Accordingly, the auxiliary verb needs to be inverted in these sentences. Please see Grammar Exercise 1 for more information on negative adverbs.

Exercise: Change the verbs given in the following sentences, using the past perfect and the simple past tense in each sentence.

1) No sooner _____ (we get) on the interstate highway than our car _____ (break down).

2) No sooner _____ (I finish) speaking on the phone than the doorbell _____ (ring).

3) Someone _____ (tell) Martha before I _____ (have) a chance.

4) Bill _____ (tear up) that note before I _____ (see) it.

5) I _____ (see) the wedding dress you _____ (choose).

6) She _____ (receive) the letter several days after I _____ (mail) it.

7) No sooner _____ (the fire start) than the alarm _____ (go off).

8) After Jim _____ (become) sleepy, he _____ (leave) the party.

9) Just when the party _____ (begin), we _____ (see) Nancy come in the door.

10) I _____ (just say) goodbye to Sally when Mary _____ (arrive).

Grammar Exercise 3: Prepositions

Many nouns, verbs, and adjectives are used with only one particular preposition. The following exercises are intended as a review of preposition usage.

Look at the following examples:
   . . . the movie script . . . is procured <u>from</u> . . .
   They must refrain <u>from</u> . . .
   The camera crew works <u>in</u> close cooperation <u>with</u> . .
   Its success ultimately lies <u>with</u> . . .

Exercise: Place the appropriate preposition in the space provided.

1) After 25 years _____ marriage, Jane is faithful _____ her husband and devoted _____ her children.
2) It took him several months to recover _____ his viral infection.
3) The politician was completely devoid _____ integrity.
4) The subject of building a new motel is currently _____ discussion.
5) I was given a perfume set for my birthday, consisting _____ a bottle of spray and lotion.
6) She was really pleased _____ receiving first prize.
7) The success of any business is contingent _____ the strength of its management.
8) He hadn't expected such an icy reception. In fact, he was really taken _____ surprise.
9) You will never be healthy if your diet is deficient _____ vitamins.
10) Police officers are _____ duty all day long.
11) Could you give me a little help _____ my chemistry assignment?
12) She had gained so much weight that she was really ashamed _____ herself.
13) The manager will investigate the matter and will contact you _____ writing.
14) She fell _____ him the moment they first met.
15) That author is famous _____ his horror stories.
16) It has taken me a long time to get accustomed _____ living in this area.
17) She really loves her car and would hate to part _____ it.
18) Many species are threatened _____ extinction nowadays.

19) If you refuse to work hard, your endeavors will amount _____ nothing.

20) I hope you're going to stand _____ your promise.

21) She is really pleased _____ her children for being so cooperative.

22) After many years as friends, the two of them finally fell _____ love.

23) Many homes in California are not insured _____ earthquake damage.

24) Will you exchange your old car _____ a different model?

25) His version of the story was not consistent _____ the facts.

26) You will be given a refund in accordance _____ the terms _____ the product warranty.

27) During the war, many soldiers were subjected _____ torture in enemy camps.

28) I don't approve _____ your behavior.

29) I haven't been introduced _____ him, although I know him _____ sight.

30) Robert's company has always operated _____ a profit.

Grammar Exercise 4: Review of Gerunds and Infinitives

Exercise: Complete the following sentences using either the gerund or infinitive form of the verb provided. If you need further help, please refer back to the gerund and infinitive section of the study guide.

1) It's not worth (write) the whole letter over again.

2) She refused (listen) to what we had to say.

3) He denied (steal) the stereo.

4) She is in the habit of (stay up) quite late.

5) I advise you (study) more.

6) He was just about (leave) when the telephone rang.

7) Sorry! I meant (tell) you about the party last week.

8) How about (go) to the movies tonight?

9) I always have trouble (tie) this necktie.

10) As manager, my job is checking (see) that you carry out your responsibilities.

11) The pianist is paid (play) music for the customers.

12) I have been thinking about (visit) my grandma on Memorial Day.

13) She really enjoys (swim) in the summer.

14) It's time (pack) our things and head home.

15) There's no reason (cry) over spilled milk.

16) I'm really tired of (hear) him complain all the time.

17) Have you ever considered (cut) your hair short?

18) I hope (win) the lottery and live in Brazil someday.

19) Imagine (have) a million dollars!

20) All passengers must prepare (land) by fastening their seat belts.

Grammar Exercise 5: "So" and "Such"

When "so" and "such" are used as modifiers for adjectives, the word order is as follows:

"so" + adjective + a(n) + noun

"such" + a(n) + adjective + noun

Look at the following example:

Not all banks impose such a harsh requirement, however.

This sentence could be re-written as follows:

Not all banks impose so harsh a requirement, however.

Exercise: Re-write the following sentences, replacing "so" with "such" and vice-versa.

1) I have never seen such an awful movie.

2) The company rarely interviews so qualified a candidate.

3) Seldom has so beautiful a painting been displayed in this gallery.

4) The scholarship has never been given to such a deserving pupil.

5) Cindy is so graceful a model that she won the beauty pageant.

6) Anna is such a sensitive person that you have to be careful about what you say to her.

7) Never have I seen such a terrible display of idiocy.

8) He is so slovenly a person that his home is a mess.

9) Sam is so huge an egomaniac that he thinks only of himself.

10) It's the first time I've had to endure such an enervating experience.

Grammar Exercise 6: Phrasal Verbs – Part 1

Phrasal verbs consist of a verb and one or more particles, which may be prepositions or adverbs. Phrasal verbs may be transitive (that is, they take an object) or intransitive (they do not take an object). Transitive phrasal verbs may be separable (the object may be placed before the particle) or inseparable (the object must be placed after the particle).

Look at these examples:

The gills must also be <u>looked at</u> to determine whether the fish can breathe freely. (EXAMINED)

Dung must be <u>disposed of</u> on a regular basis to ensure proper hygiene. (REMOVED)

Exercise: Place the missing particle or particles in the phrasal verbs provided in the following sentences. A definition is given to help you.

1) I ran _____ her at the mall yesterday. (ENCOUNTERED)

2) I'm not dating him anymore. We broke_____ two weeks ago. (FINISH A RELATIONSHIP)

3) What's the point of trying? I give_____ ! (SURRENDER)

4) She has taken _____ the management of the corporation. (TAKEN CONTROL OF)

5) I'm kind of old-fashioned because I was brought _____ by my grand-parents. (RAISED)

6) Our pick-up truck broke _____ in the middle of the road. (CEASED TO FUNCTION)

7) We waved good-bye from the terminal as the airplane took _____ . (ASCENDED)

8) The nurse tried to bring her _____ after she fainted. (HELP TO REGAIN CONSCIOUSNESS)

9) I don't see how he got _____ _____ cheating on the final exam. (REMAINED FREE FROM BLAME)

10) The majority of the runners could not keep _____ _____ the leader in the marathon. (MAINTAIN THE PACE)

11) Car alarms that give _____ those squealing noises really annoy me. (EMIT)

12) The salary and benefits package your company has offered me is quite generous. I would, however, like a few days to think the matter _____ . (CONTEMPLATE)

13) After further consideration, I have decided to turn _____ your offer. (REJECT)

14) Where is Jaime? I wonder if he got held _____ in traffic somewhere. (DELAYED)

15) First, his wife left him. Then, his company went bankrupt, and now all his friends have turned _____ him. (BETRAYED)

16) He must be the most benevolent man on earth. He is always giving money _____ to charity. (CONTRIBUTING)

17) I'd advise you to steer clear of her. You'll only have trouble if you get mixed _____ in her affairs. (GET INVOLVED)

18) The baseball game was put _____ until Friday due to the rain. (POSTPONED)

19) It's taken you forever to get _____ your cold. (RECOVER)

20) I wasn't ready to get up when my alarm clock went _____ this morning. (SOUNDED)

21) Have you heard the news? War may break _____ overseas. (OCCUR)

22) If the snow would hold _____ for a few days, they could clear a pass through the mountains. (CEASE TEMPORARILY)

23) The government should do something about the current rate of inflation. Prices are perpetually going _____ . (INCREASING)

24) You need to cut _____ _____ your intake of saturated fat or you'll have a heart attack. (REDUCE)

25) He told me to look him _____ if I'm ever in Dallas on business. (LOCATE)

26) Their plans for a two-week vacation in the Caribbean fell _____ at the last minute. (FAILED TO MATERIALIZE)

27) You're an imbecile if you believe that story! She's made the whole thing _____ ! (INVENTED, CREATED)

28) He constantly belittles her. He always makes her feel inferior by putting her _____ . (CRITICIZING)

29) I can't stay at your place all week. I don't want to put you _____ . (IMPOSE)

30) You're free to go now. We won't take _____ any more of your time. (USE, WASTE)

Grammar Exercise 7: The Definite Article – "The"

The definite article is used in the following ways:

1) If it is not the first time that something is mentioned in the conversation.

    EXAMPLE: My son goes to school. In fact, he goes to the school just around the corner.

2) To show emphasis or disbelief.

    EXAMPLE: – I saw George Clooney at the Seven-11!
    – Certainly not the George Clooney!

3) If the thing being mentioned is one of a kind.

    EXAMPLE: We stayed at the Athens Hilton on vacation.

4) With the names rivers, oceans, and mountain ranges, but not with the names of cities, towns, or states.

    EXAMPLE: The Rocky Mountains are located in Colorado.

5) With the names of countries consisting of different nations or states and with groups of islands.

    EXAMPLE: She is a citizen of the United States.

6) To refer to groups or classes of people.

    EXAMPLE: He always gives money to the poor.

7) When the speaker is discussing something in particular, rather than in general.

    EXAMPLE: The music at their wedding reception was atrocious.

8) Before the word "hospital." (**NOTE**: This particular usage is different than British English.)

    EXAMPLE: My friend was in the hospital last week.

9) With the names of seasons. (**NOTE** This usage is also different than British English.)

    EXAMPLE: I enjoy swimming in the summer.

Look at this example:

> Some have argued that if the health care system cannot provide care for those who need it most, namely the feeble and frail, it is of no real use whatsoever.

"The" is used because the writer is speaking about a certain group of people, the feeble and frail. In other words, this sentence is similar to example 6 above.

Exercise: Complete the following sentences, adding the definite article where appropriate. Note that some gaps do not require an article.

1) A few hillbillies still live in _____ Appalachian Mountains.

2) The government should allocate more funds to programs for _____ elderly.

3) He is going to _____ college in _____ fall.

4) Her fiancé is from _____ Texas.

5) _____ movie I saw last night was fantastic.

6) I really don't care for _____ country and western music.

7) _____ President lives in _____ White House.

8) My brother is in _____ hospital with a severe case of appendicitis.

9) There are a lot of barges on _____ Mississippi River, especially near _____ St. Louis.

10) Right! You saw _____ Brad Pitt at the gas station!

11) We went to _____ Italy and _____ Greek Islands on vacation last year.

12) Is she from _____ France or _____ United Kingdom?

13) Have you ever seen _____ Great Salt Lake in _____ Utah?

14) – Did you knit that sweater?

    – No, it's _____ sweater I bought at Macy's in _____ New York.

15) _____ Buffalo Bills have just won _____ Super Bowl.

Grammar Exercise 8: Comparatives and Superlatives

The comparative form is used to compare two people or things from the same group or category.

EXAMPLE: Maria is the nicer of the two sisters.
(In this example, Maria and her sister form one group.)

The comparative form is also used to compare a person or thing to a group from which it is considered separate.

EXAMPLE: Maria is nicer than her three sisters.
(There are four sisters. Maria is in one category. The three remaining sisters are in another category.)

The superlative form is used to compare a person or thing to a group from which it is considered a member.

EXAMPLE: Maria is the nicest of her four sisters.
(All four sisters are considered to be in the same category.)

NOTES:
a) Remember to use the definite article ("the") with the superlative.
b) Double comparatives and double superlatives are grammatically incorrect.

WRONG: She is more prettier than her sister.
WRONG: She is the most prettiest in the family.

Look at this example:

Stories about the exploration of the American frontier have become more popular than fables or nursery rhymes.

Stories about the frontier are considered to be in one category. Fables and nursery rhymes are in another.

Exercise: Complete the sentences with the comparative or superlative form of the given adjective. You must add "the," "of," and "than" when necessary.

1. Professor Smith is _____ man I know.   INTELLIGENT

2. Professor Smith is _____ any other man I know.   INTELLIGENT

3. Nancy is _____ her five sisters.   BEAUTIFUL

4. Nancy is _____ the five sisters.   BEAUTIFUL

5. Nathan is _____ boy in his class.   SMART

6. Nathan is _____ the other boys in his class.   SMART

7. They promoted her to manager because she worked _____ the other employees.   HARD

8. They promoted her to manager because she worked _____ all the employees.   HARD

9. Beth is _____ any other girl on the volleyball team.   TALL

10. Beth is _____ girl on the volleyball team.   TALL

Grammar Exercise 9: The Third Conditional

The third conditional is used to hypothesize, or make a guess about, how a past event could have happened differently. The following structure is used:

> If + past perfect . . . would + have + past participle

The past perfect structure is sometimes inverted on the examination. This involves removing the word "if" from the sentence and beginning the sentence with the word "had."

Look at this example:

> <u>Had</u> these duplicitous politicians <u>been</u> aware of the menace posed by such journalists, they <u>would have been</u> much more careful in carrying out their subterfuge.

This sentence has been inverted. It could be re-written as follows:

> <u>If</u> these duplicitous politicians <u>had been</u> aware of the menace posed by such journalists, they <u>would have been</u> more careful in carrying out their subterfuge.

Exercise: Write one sentence for each of the following groups of sentences, using the inverted third conditional structure. You may need to add or remove the word "not" from either clause of the sentence you make.

1) Marek didn't drive carefully. He had an accident.

   Had Marek . . .

2) Pavel decided not to buy the car. She didn't like it.

   Had Pavel . . .

3) I didn't pass my exam. I didn't study for it.

   Had I . . .

4) Dasha didn't wear a sweater. She caught a cold.

   Had Dasha . . .

5) I didn't prepare anything to eat. I didn't know you were coming.

   Had I . . .

6) Zahra was so bored by the TV program. She fell asleep.

   Had Zahra . . .

7) The movie wasn't interesting. I left half-way through.

   Had the movie . . .

8) I told my friend he was stupid. He left in a rage.

   Had I not . . .

9) He argued with his boss. As a result, he was fired.

   Had he not . . .

10) It rained all night. The football game was canceled.

    Had it not . . .

Grammar Exercise 10: Phrasal Verbs – Part 2

This section is intended as an additional review of phrasal verb usage. *Look at these examples:*

Recording artists sometimes <u>start off</u> by writing their own songs.

A specimen recording, called a demo, is made initially to <u>check out</u> the sound quality and viability of the artist.

    start off = commence
    check out = verify

Exercise: Match the underlined phrasal verb in each sentence on the left to the correct meaning provided on the right. Note that this exercise is continued on the following pages.

PART A

1. She just <u>barged into</u> the room without knocking.
2. We all <u>chipped in</u> to buy Aisha a birthday present.
3. He is really very shy, but if you get to know him, you may <u>hit it off</u>.
4. They are going to <u>knock down</u> the old movie theater next week.
5. They are <u>turning</u> their garage <u>into</u> a family room.
6. Do you know where I can <u>get a hold of</u> yesterday's newspaper?
7. I really hate college, but I've decided to <u>stick it out</u>.
8. Running that marathon really <u>did</u> me <u>in</u>.
9. I really <u>look up to</u> you for your courage.
10. I can ignore you error this time but don't <u>slip up</u> again.

A. to be compatible
B. to convert
C. to enter without knocking
D. to endure
E. to admire
F. to acquire
G. to contribute
H. to cause physical exhaustion
I. to make a mistake
J. to demolish

PART B

1. Raquel is far from taciturn. In fact, she can really <u>ramble on</u>. A. to misbehave

2. None of the students knew what the professor was <u>driving at</u>. B. to locate with difficulty

3. The teacher was angry because we were <u>fooling around</u> in class. C. to create a negative state of health

4. You <u>bring on</u> most of your problems by yourself. D. to cease

5. Newspaper reporters are always trying to <u>dig up</u> gossip. E. to cause

6. That really annoys me. I wish you would <u>cut it out</u>. F. to disapprove of something

7. If you don't stop working so hard you will <u>run</u> yourself <u>down</u>. G. to revoke

8. Smoking in the hospital cafeteria is <u>frowned on</u>. H. to talk incessantly

9. I thought I wasn't going to like the party, but it <u>turned out</u> to be a lot of fun. I. to result in

10. I hope you won't <u>go back on</u> your promise to help me. J. to mean something

PART C

1. Enrique <u>bailed out of</u> the agreement after having second thoughts.
2. The baseball game was <u>called off</u> due to the rain.
3. Why do you <u>keep on</u> doing that? I've told you a million times to stop.
4. Julia didn't <u>let on</u> that she knew about the surprise party.
5. I enjoy <u>looking through</u> all kinds of magazines, especially *The Scientific American*.
6. He is such a bully. He should <u>pick on</u> somebody his own size for a change.
7. You can <u>pick out</u> any of the tomatoes you like.
8. Be ready at 8:00 sharp. I'll <u>pick</u> you <u>up</u> at the front door.
9. She is going to <u>try out</u> for the marching band next week.
10. You shouldn't <u>take on</u> more responsibilities than you can handle.

A. to withdraw from
B. to peruse
C. to choose
D. to audition
E. to betray a secret
F. to provide transportation
G. to persist
H. to tease or torment
I. to accept
J. to cancel

ANSWERS:

GRAMMAR 1

1) Not until noon would bread be available at the grocery store. Type 1

2) Only when his truck ran out of gas did Frank realize he had forgotten to fill it up. Type 4

3) Never before have I changed a flat tire. Type 3

4) Only when he took off his sunglasses did I realize who he was. Type 4

5) Never in my life have I seen such an exciting football game. Type 3

6) Not a word did John say during the entire drive home. Type 3

7) Rarely does a teenager flunk his driving test the first time. Types 2 and 5

8) Seldom does Jane stay out past midnight. Type 5

9) Only once have I seen the Grand Canyon. Type 1

10) Hardly ever does he have time to see his parents since he is away at college. Types 2 and 5

GRAMMAR 2

1) No sooner had we gotten on the interstate highway than our car broke down.

2) No sooner had I finished speaking on the telephone than the doorbell rang.

3) Someone had told Martha before I had a chance.

4) Bill had torn up that note before I saw it.

5) I saw the wedding dress you had chosen.

6) She received the letter several days after I had mailed it.

7) No sooner had the fire started than the alarm went off.

8) After Jim had become sleepy, he left the party.

9) Just when the party had begun, we saw Nancy come in the door.

10) I had just said goodbye to Sally when Mary arrived.

GRAMMAR 3

1) of, to, to

2) from

3) of

4) under

5) of

6) about

7) upon or on

8) by

9) in

10) on

11) with

12) of

13) in

14) for

15) for

16) to

17) with

18) with

19) to

20) by

21) with

22) in

23) for

24) for

25) with

26) with, of

27) to

28) of

29) to, by

30) at

GRAMMAR 4

1) writing

2) to listen

3) stealing

4) staying up

5) to study

6) to leave

7) to tell

8) going

9) tying

10) to see

11) to play

12) visiting

13) swimming

14) to pack

15) to cry

16) hearing

17) cutting

18) to win

19) having

20) to land

GRAMMAR 5

1) so awful a movie

2) such a qualified candidate

3) such a beautiful painting

4) so deserving a pupil

5) such a graceful model

6) so sensitive a person

7) so terrible a display

8) such a slovenly person

9) such a huge egomaniac

10) so enervating an experience

GRAMMAR 6

1) into

2) up

3) up

4) over

5) up

6) down

7) off

8) around

9) away with

10) up with

11) off

12) over

13) down

14) up

15) against

16) away

17) up

18) off

19) over

20) off

21) out

22) up

23) up

24) down on

25) up

26) through

27) up

28) down

29) out

30) up

GRAMMAR 7

1) the

2) the

3) --, the

4) --

5) The

6) --

7) The, the

8) the

9) the, --

10) the

11) --, the

12) --, the

13) the, --

14) the, --

15) The, the

GRAMMAR 8

1) the most intelligent

2) more intelligent than

3) more beautiful than

4) the most beautiful of

5) the smartest

6) smarter than

7) harder than

8) the hardest of

9) taller than

10) the tallest

GRAMMAR 9

1) Had Marek driven more carefully, he wouldn't have had an accident.

2) Had Pavel liked the car, she would have bought it.

3) Had I studied for my exam, I would have passed it.

4) Had Dasha worn a sweater, she wouldn't have caught a cold.

5) Had I known you were coming, I would have prepared something to eat.

6) Had Zahra not been so bored by the TV program, she wouldn't have fallen asleep.

7) Had the movie been interesting, I wouldn't have left half-way through.

8) Had I not told my friend he was stupid, he wouldn't have left in a rage.

9) Had he not argued with his boss, he wouldn't have been fired.

10) Had it not rained all night, the football game wouldn't have been canceled.

GRAMMAR 10

PART A

1) C

2) G

3) A

4) J

5) B

6) F

7) D

8) H

9) E

10) I

PART B

1) H

2) J

3) A

4) E

5) B

6) D

7) C

8) F

9) I

10) G

PART C

1) A

2) J

3) G

4) E

5) B

6) H

7) C

8) F

9) D

10) I

Part 3 - Accuplacer ESL LOEP Idiom List

The following idioms may appear on the Accuplacer ESL test. You may therefore wish to study this list before taking the practice tests in this book. (sthg = something; sbdy = somebody)

apply oneself - to work very hard on a specific task. e.g. - If we <u>apply ourselves</u>, we should be able to clean up the house in two hours.

as hard as nails - relating to a person who is strong and determined. e.g. - He won't give up. He's <u>as hard as nails</u>.

be a wreck - to be in very bad physical condition, esp. from nervousness or exhaustion. e.g. - She is a <u>wreck</u> from worrying about her upcoming hospital stay.

be caught red-handed - to be discovered during the commission of criminal activities. e.g. - He was <u>caught red-handed</u> as he attempted to put the stolen merchandise in his pocket.

be in ruins - to be totally destroyed. e.g. - The town was <u>in ruins</u> after the hurricane.

be of strong moral fiber - to be of good moral character. e.g. - He would never lie or steal. He is <u>of strong moral fiber</u>.

beating around the bush - to avoid talking about a certain topic. e.g. - I tried to get an answer out of her, but she kept on <u>beating around the bush</u>.

beside yourself - to be very nervous or upset. e.g. - I am just <u>beside myself</u> waiting for the results of my test.

beyond my wildest dreams - to be better than your highest expectations. e.g. - My vacation in Rome was <u>beyond my wildest dreams</u>.

blow your chances - to lose all opportunities for success in an activity. e.g. - He <u>blew his chances</u> of buying a car by losing all his money gambling.

blue - relating to extreme sadness or depression. e.g. - She felt <u>blue</u> after her boyfriend left her. I've never seen her so down.

bored to tears - very bored. e.g. - The lesson was hardly interesting. In fact, I was <u>bored to tears</u>.

box office - the cashier's office at a movie theater. e.g. - We bought our tickets at the movie theater <u>box office</u>.

buck - dollar. e.g. - I bought this sweater for twelve <u>bucks</u>.

butter sbdy up - to win someone's favor through flattery. e.g. - He tried to <u>butter me up</u> by saying how beautiful I looked today.

by leaps and bounds - with incredible or amazing speed. e.g. - The world population crisis is evident in countries such as India, where the population has grown <u>by leaps and bounds</u>.

call for sthg - to make something necessary or required. e.g. - This recipe <u>calls for</u> white wine.

cast aspersions on sbdy's character - to damage someone's reputation through rumors or gossip. e.g. - I would never <u>cast aspersions on his character</u>. In fact, I know that he is a very nice person.

cheat on - to be unfaithful to one's spouse or romantic partner. e.g. - He is filing for divorce because his wife was <u>cheating</u> on him.

check sthg out - to look at or verify something. e.g. - <u>Check out</u> the story in this newspaper. It's really amazing.

checkered past - to have undesirable experiences in one's past. e.g. - He doesn't speak about his life in Chicago. He must <u>have a checkered past</u>.

count me in - I want to participate in the activity. e.g. - I'll come to the party with you. <u>Count me in</u>.

crack sbdy up - to amuse someone. e.g. - His funny jokes really <u>crack me up</u>.

crushed - to be very disappointed. e.g. - She was <u>crushed</u> when her boyfriend left her.

cut off your nose to spite your face - to hurt oneself by seeking revenge on others. e.g. - I know that you don't like your teacher, but telling her that she's stupid was <u>cutting off your nose to spite your face</u>.

dig up - to discover as a result of searching extensively. e.g. - He searched through his closet, trying to <u>dig up</u> something to wear.

don't rain on my parade - don't discourage me. e.g. - I just know I'm going to win the lottery so <u>don't rain on my parade</u>!

drive a hard bargain - to be difficult to negotiate with. e.g. - He's not going to change his mind. He <u>drives a hard bargain</u>.

drop a hint - to give someone subtle ideas about something in order to express one's likes or dislikes. e.g. - He <u>dropped a hint</u> that he would like a new tie for his birthday.

drop in - to visit someone's home without having arranged a specific time. e.g. - <u>Drop in</u> and see me sometime!

face the music - to accept reality. e.g. - <u>Face the music</u>! You are never going to win the lottery.

fair-weather friend - loyal only during times of good fortune. e.g. - Don't trust him. He's a <u>fair-weather</u> friend.

feel together - to feel organized and well. e.g. - She can't be <u>feeling together</u> today after the way she drank at the party last night.

fizzle out - to reduce gradually in amount or quality. e.g. - Interest in our exercise class has <u>fizzled out</u>. There are only two students left.

flat broke - to be completely out of money. e.g. - He is <u>flat broke</u> and is considering filing for bankruptcy.

flirt with disaster - to become involved in a dangerous or risky situation. e.g. - Every time you drive over the speed limit, you are just <u>flirting with disaster</u>.

flog a dead horse - to speak so much about a particular topic that others become bored or fed up. e.g. - She is always talking about failing her exams. Talk about <u>flogging a dead horse</u>.

for all intents and purposes - for all practical purposes; in effect, though not in fact. e.g. - My computer is useless <u>for all intents and purposes</u> since I cannot use new software on it.

for keeps - to take possession or ownership of sthg forever. e.g. - He gave me a diamond ring for keeps.

fresh out of sthg - to have exhausted the supply of something. e.g. - We are fresh out of grapefruit today. You'll need to come back again tomorrow.

get along like cats and dogs - to be entirely incompatible. e.g. - I can't live with my mother. We get along like cats and dogs.

get in touch - to get in contact with someone. e.g. - Get in touch with me next week. You can telephone me at home.

get on sbdy's good side - to win someone's favor. e.g. - He tried to get on the teacher's good side by bringing her gifts.

get the lowdown on something - to obtain secret or inside information about something. e.g. - Did you get the lowdown? I heard a rumor that the factory is going to close.

give sbdy a lift - to give someone a ride in your car. e.g. - Can you give me a lift into town?

give sbdy the creeps - to frighten someone. e.g. - Horror movies give me the creeps.

give sbdy a break - to stop giving harsh treatment to an individual. e.g. - You mean that you won't help me? Why won't somebody just give me a break?

grab a bite - to go for a meal, esp. quickly. e.g. - Let's grab a bite for lunch.

grasping at straws - to try many alternative solutions in desperation. e.g. - You don't know the answer to the homework so now you're grasping at straws.

green - inexperienced; without knowledge. e.g. - He is green since today is his first day on the job and he has no previous experience.

grow on - to get used to. e.g. - I didn't like my new school too much at first, but it has started to grow on me.

handle sthg - to endure or tolerate something. e.g. - I just can't handle waking up so early in the morning.

happy-go-lucky - carefree. e.g. - He's so happy-go-lucky that you'd think he didn't have a care in the world.

have a one-track mind - to only have one thing on your mind. e.g. - Paula has a one-track mind. All she ever thinks about is money.

have pull - to be influential. e.g. - I think Raphael can get us tickets for the game on Sunday. He has pull with the team.

He made his bed, and now he can lie in it. – a person must face the consequences of his actions. e.g. - It was his own decision to cheat on the exam. Now that he got caught, I can only say that he made his bed, and now he can lie in it.

heard it through the grapevine - to hear people talking or gossiping about a certain topic or subject. e.g. - I wasn't told the news about the situation directly. I heard it through the grapevine.

hit the nail on the head - to make an appropriate remark or statement. e.g. - The politician hit the nail on the head when he said that more financial aid should be offered to students.

Hit the road! - Go away. Leave me alone. (syn.) Take a hike! e.g. - A strange man was bothering me in the mall so I told him to hit the road.

hit the spot - That was just what I was craving. e.g. - Lemonade really hits the spot on a hot summer day.

hold a grudge - to bear resentment towards another person. e.g. - Julia is still holding a grudge because I criticized her work.

hold your tongue - to keep one's opinions to oneself. e.g. - I wanted to tell her off, but I held my tongue.

holding the bag - to be forced to take an action or make a decision. e.g. - He didn't help me as he promised and left me holding the bag.

hop in - get inside my car. e.g. - I'll take you to the store. Hop in.

How come? - Why? e.g. - She's not going out tonight. How come?

in the red - to have a negative numerical balance. e.g. - The company had to close down after operating in the red for months.

It doesn't hold water - it's not believable. e.g. - I don't believe him. His story doesn't hold water.

It was a hit - it was very popular or a huge success. e.g. - The rock group's new song was a huge hit.

It was a piece of cake - it was very easy. e.g. - The exam was a piece of cake. I'm sure I passed.

It's old hat - it's old news. e.g. - Everyone knows that. It's old hat.

jot down - to write quickly in note form. e.g. - He jotted down the number that I gave him over the telephone.

keep in touch - to stay in contact with someone through telephone calls or correspondence. e.g. - Although my best friend lives miles away, we still manage to keep in touch.

Keep it down! - Be quiet! e.g. - Keep it down in there! I'm trying to study!

keep sbdy posted - to keep someone informed. e.g. - We expect to hear some news next week, so we'll keep you posted.

keep a lid on it - to keep something a secret. e.g. - I'll tell you a secret if you can keep a lid on it.

let it slip - to divulge secret information. e.g. - That was supposed to be a secret, but she let it slip.

let the cat out of the bag - to divulge secret information. e.g. - I told her not to tell anyone, but she let the cat out of the bag.

lighten up - to relax. You'd better learn to lighten up or you'll have a heart attack.

like looking for a needle in a haystack - to search for something that has many possible locations. e.g. - Searching for our lost keys on the beach was like looking for a needle in a haystack.

make heads or tails of sthg - to attempt to understand something with difficulty. e.g. - I can't make heads or tails of this map. Do you know which road to take?

make yourself scarce - not to keep one's normal company as the result of a situation which has caused conflict. e.g. - I haven't seen her in weeks. She has made herself scarce.

make the big time - the highest level of success of a project or venture. e.g. - An actor is considered to have made the big time when he stars in a leading role.

make the grade - to have an acceptable standard of performance. e.g. - I didn't get to play in the game because I couldn't make the grade.

mouth off - to be rude or impudent. e.g. - You should be punished for mouthing off to your parents.

nitpick - to be overly concerned with very small details. e.g. - My boss is very demanding and nitpicks the smallest details.

nitwit - an idiot; a stupid person. e.g. - If you don't know that two and two equals four, you are a bigger nitwit than I thought.

no "if's", "and's" or "but's" - no excuses will be accepted. e.g. - You will do your homework - no "if's", "and's" or "but's"!

on schedule - to be on time. e.g. - The bus is on schedule today. We should get to work on time.

once in a blue moon - something that happens very rarely. e.g. - I don't like bowling and go only once in a blue moon.

out of the question – something that is impossible even to consider. e.g. - Going on vacation this year is out of the question. We just don't have enough money.

overstay one's welcome - to stay longer than one is welcome; to begin to impose upon one's host. e.g. - It was obvious that we had overstayed our welcome when she asked us if we would leave her house as soon as possible.

pick a fight - to encourage a physical attack by displaying a hostile attitude. e.g. - He picked a fight by saying that I was too weak to hit him.

picked over - being of limited variety because other individuals have already chosen the best items. e.g. - The fruit at the grocery store was picked over because we arrived too late in the day.

pin your hopes on sthg - to be very hopeful that something will happen. e.g. - I wouldn't pin your hopes on being accepted into medical school. You know how tough the competition is.

pinch pennies - to be very economical with money or in spending. e.g. - He is pinching pennies because he lost his job last month.

play with fire - to become involved in a dangerous situation. e.g. - If you decide to cheat on the test, you're really playing with fire.

pricey - very expensive. e.g. - They can eat at that pricey restaurant because they have a lot of money.

pull through - to survive an accident or illness. e.g. - The doctors say that he will pull through his accident.

put yourself in my shoes - to try to understand the situation another person is in. e.g. - If you'd put yourself in my shoes, you would understand why I did what I had to do.

recover with flying colors - to recover very well after an accident or injury. e.g. - She is recovering with flying colors after her operation and should be out of the hospital by the weekend.

red tape - complications or paperwork involved in government procedures or bureaucracy. e.g. - Applying for a job with the government involves a lot of red tape.

resign yourself to a situation - to accept a bad situation and stop attempting to change it for the better. e.g. - She used to hate living with her mother-in-law, but has finally resigned herself to the situation.

ring a bell - to sound familiar. e.g. - Now that you mention it, that story does ring a bell.

search high and low - to search for something extensively. e.g. - I've searched high and low for my car keys, but I still can't find them.

set sbdy straight - to point out a mistake in another person's behavior or thinking. e.g. - I need to set you straight. The bus leaves at 3:00, not 3:30.

set the record straight - to provide someone with correct information after they have been misinformed. e.g. - I want to set the record straight. I paid $2 for the tickets, not $20.

shape up or ship out - improve your behavior or you will be forced to leave. e.g. - Do your job properly or be fired. In other words, shape up or ship out!

shed light on sthg - to explain. e.g. - Could you shed some light on this homework?

show sbdy the ropes - to provide someone with instructions. e.g. - He showed me the ropes on my first day of work.

skeletons in your closet - to hide secrets about your past. e.g. - She doesn't talk a lot about her past. I wonder if she has skeletons in her closet.

size up - to make an estimation of or decision about the value or worth of something; (syn.) evaluate. e.g. - The town's people sized up the damage caused by the earthquake.

spill the beans - to divulge secret information. e.g. - She spilled the beans about all the confidential information that I had told her.

spin a yarn - to tell a story, esp. a long one. He was really spinning a yarn. I thought he would never stop talking!

spring up - to appear quickly or unexpectedly from a specific source. e.g. - A leak suddenly sprang up from the water pipe.

steer clear of - to avoid. e.g. - If you steer clear of the dangerous areas when you are in New York City, you shouldn't have any problem.

sthg under your hat - to hide a secret. e.g. - I don't trust him. He has something under his hat.

sthg up your sleeve - to hide information about something. e.g. - Is that all you wanted to tell me or do you have something up your sleeve?

stick to your guns - not changing one's mind or opinion. e.g. - He won't change his mind because he always sticks to his guns.

stood up - to have an appointment or a date broken by someone. e.g. - I was supposed to meet her at 10:00, but she stood me up.

stumbling block - something that prevents or hinders progress. (syn.) hindrance, obstacle, barrier. e.g. - His poor health was a stumbling block towards his performance at work.

sweet tooth - to enjoy eating sweets very much. e.g. - She has a sweet tooth and enjoys eating cake and candy.

take its/their toll - to begin to affect, esp. negatively. e.g. - Missing several nights of sleep finally took its toll on him.

talk a mile a minute - to talk very quickly. e.g. - It is difficult to understand him. He talks a mile a minute.

That takes the cake! - that is shocking or unbelievable. e.g. - He asked to borrow money from you again. That really takes the cake!

That's the way the cookie crumbles - That's life. e.g. - I just lost ten dollars. Oh well, that's the way the cookie crumbles.

toe the line - to conform to a rigid standard of behavior. e.g. - If you want to lose ten pounds in two weeks, you will have to toe the line.

touch base - to come into contact or communicate with. e.g. - I will touch base with you next week concerning the status of the contract.

touchy - overly sensitive or moody. e.g. - She is touchy and hates being criticized.

turn on a dime - to have great flexibility in motion. e.g. - This car is one of the finest machines I have ever driven. It can turn on a dime.

turn over a new leaf - to improve one's behavior; to change for the better. e.g. - The student promised to turn over a new leaf and start handing in his homework on time.

under the weather - to feel sick or generally unwell. e.g. – My father feels under the weather and has been in bed for four days.

up to doing sthg - to be in the mood to do something. e.g. - I'm not up to going out tonight. Let's stay home.

you can count on it - you can depend on it; it is certain to happen. e.g. - You can count on her coming to the party. She promised to be there.

PART 4 - Reading Comprehension Tips

There are four types of questions on the reading comprehension test for the Accuplacer ESL.

The questions are on reading passages, which are followed by multiple choice questions containing four choices each.

The questions may be placed into the following categories:

a) Questions asking you to identify the main idea of the passage

For this type of question, you have to ignore answer choices that give specific points mentioned in the passage.

b) Questions asking you to decide what can be inferred from the passage

Infer means to understand something that has not been directly stated or explained.

These types of questions are asking you to "read between the lines" of the passage and draw conclusions.

c) Questions asking you about some specific detail in the passage

For this type of question, be sure you choose a specific answer.

You should ignore answer choices that cover the main idea of the passage or that give general information.

d) Application questions that ask you to determine the author's purpose

You should look carefully for adjectives in the passage that describe the author's point of view.

Part 5 - Essay Topics

The following essay topics are provided as examples of the types of prompts you may see on the Writeplacer ESL essay examination.

If you need further help with essay writing, you may be interested in our other publication entitled: *Writeplacer Success: Accuplacer Essay Writing Guide*

1) Many people are of the opinion that professional athletes are overpaid. Write a balanced discussion on this topic, including the reasons for and against this belief.

2) Children become dependent upon television for entertainment from a very early age. Please explain this phenomenon.

3) What qualities and skills should a good teacher possess? Explain and give examples.

4) Write a balanced discussion on the advantages and disadvantages of compulsory military service.

5) Televisions programs are often filled with scenes of violence. These depictions will lead to an increase in violent crimes in society. Do you agree or disagree? Why?

6) Describe the car you would most like to own.

7) "Capital punishment acts as an effective deterrent to crime." Do you agree or disagree? Why?

8) Would you raise your children in the same way that your parents have raised you? Why or why not? Discuss and give examples.

9) "The prevention of cruelty to animals is one of the most pressing concerns facing modern society." Do you agree or disagree? Why?

10) Many people engage in dangerous or unhealthy behaviors such as smoking or failing to wear seat belts, although they are fully aware of the risks involved. Please explain the reasons for this phenomenon.

11) Describe the attributes you seek in an ideal spouse.

12) "Life two hundred years ago was much more difficult than it is today." Do you agree? Why or why not?

13) "You are what you eat." Do you agree? Why or why not?

14) In America, it is common for the public to scrutinize a political candidate's personal life, including details of past and current romantic affairs. Are these

personal details relevant to a politician's professional capabilities? Why or why not?

15) Imagine that you were rich and famous. How would your life be different?

16) If you could be a professional athlete, which sport would you choose? Why?

17) "Television programs have no educational value." Discuss.

18) How should students be evaluated: according to their achievements or their effort? Discuss.

19) In certain countries, women are required to serve in the armed forces. What effect does this have on them, their families, and society?

20) Describe the funniest movie you have ever seen and explain why you enjoyed it.

21) Air pollution from automobile exhaust is an increasing threat to the environment. Please discuss the measures that your country has taken to combat this problem.

22) "The punishment should fit the crime." Discuss.

23) Describe a favorite uncle or aunt and explain why you enjoy his or her company.

24) Would you prefer to live in a large city or in a farming community in the countryside? Explain the reasons for your choice.

25) "Good health is more important than fame or fortune." Discuss.

26) "Friendship is more powerful than love." Do you agree or disagree? Why?

27) "Developments in modern technology are in many ways inimical to a healthy lifestyle." Discuss.

28) What advice would you give to someone who wants to lose weight?

29) What do you think is your country's greatest problem? Explain in detail and say what could be done to improve the situation.

30) What famous person, living or dead, do you admire most? Why?

ADVANTAGE+ EDITION BONUS MATERIAL

Additional GRAMMAR REVIEW AND PRACTICE EXERCISES

Adverbs of Place – Location

You will probably see one or two questions on adverbs of location on the grammar section of the LOEP Test.

The function of adverbs of location is to state where things happen. They are sometimes also referred to as spatial adverbs.

Adverbs of location include the following:

- anyplace
- anyplace else
- anywhere
- anywhere else
- another place
- elsewhere
- everywhere
- somewhere
- somewhere else

When using an adverb of location with "I'd rather," be sure to use one with the word "else" or "another" since you are making a comparison.

ADVERBS OF LOCATION FOR COMPARISON

Elsewhere / somewhere else / another place

These three adverbs indicate that you may have other preferences in mind, besides the location already mentioned.

Example 1:

The weather is going to be bad in New York this weekend, so I'd rather go elsewhere.

Example 2:

The weather is going to be bad in New York this weekend, so I'd rather go somewhere else.

Example 3:

The weather is going to be bad in New York this weekend, so I'd rather go another place.

Anywhere else / anyplace else

These two adverbs indicate that you don't have another preference in mind. Your mind is completely open to other ideas.

Example 4:

The weather is going to be bad in New York this weekend, so I'd rather go anywhere else.

Example 5:

The weather is going to be bad in New York this weekend, so I'd rather go anyplace else.

RMEMBER: When you use the word "else" you must be making a comparison in the sentence to another location.

ADVERBS OF LOCATION – NONCOMPARATIVE

Anyplace / anywhere / everywhere / somewhere

These adverbs are used when you are not making a comparison in the sentence.

Example 6:

I'll go anyplace you want.

I'll go anywhere you want.

Use "anyplace" when the speaker has no other preference.

Example 7:

    Your keys must be somewhere.

Use "somewhere" when you are not sure of the exact location.

Example 8:

    Pollen is everywhere this time of year.

Use "everywhere" when you want to show that the location is extremely common.

Now try the exercises on the next page.

Exercises – Adverbs of Location

Put one of the adverbs of location in the following sentences. Some sentences may have more than one correct answer. The answers to these exercises are provided at the back of the book.

anyplace / anyplace else / anywhere / anywhere else / another place / elsewhere / everywhere / somewhere / somewhere else

1) I don't know where I left my book. It could be _____.

2) Dallas is going to be so busy today. I'd rather go _____ , like Houston or Austin.

3) The doctor said the flu is very widespread this year because the virus is _____.

4) I just detest that restaurant. I'll go _____ !

5) I remember using that pair of scissors just a minute ago, so they must be _____ in the house.

6) He lost his keys when he was out, so they could be _____.

7) I don't like getting coffee in the mall, so I'd rather go _____ , like that cafe in town.

8) I dropped that pen while I was sitting at the desk, so it must be here _____ in the office.

9) I can't stand going to her house. I'd go _____ . I don't care where!

10) With these freezing temperatures, ice is _____ outside this time of year.

Adverbs of Degree

You will probably see at least one question on adverbs of degree on the grammar section of the LOEP Test.

The function of adverbs of degree is to state the intensity or degree of something.

Adverbs of degree are normally placed before the adjective or verb that they modify. However, there are some exceptions to this rule.

Here are some adverbs of degree and their rules of use.

TYPE 1: These adverbs must be placed before an adjective or adjectival phrase:

absolutely – to indicate the strongest or highest intensity of feeling

    I felt absolutely intimidated at that job interview.

    She was absolutely in love with him.

quite – to indicate a weaker intensity of feeling

    That movie was quite good, but I preferred the one we saw last week.

TYPE 2: The following adverbs must be placed before an adjective. They can also be used to modify a verb.

almost – to indicate that something is nearly complete

    The meal was almost ready.

    We have almost finished putting up wallpaper in our dining room.

barely – to indicate that something has only just been achieved.

    She was barely ten years old when her mother died.

    We could barely hear what the teacher was saying.

even – to intensify consequences or outcomes

> Your letter wasn't even professional because it had so many mistakes.

> Your lack of studying might even cause you to fail the exam.

hardly – to indicate the negative. Usage is similar to the word "not."

> Your lack of interest in me is hardly endearing.

> This small room can hardly be called a suite.

nearly – to indicate that something almost happened. Similar to "almost."

> The meal was nearly ready.

> We have nearly finished putting up wallpaper in our dining room.

EXCEPTIONS:

far – requires a comparative adjective

> It would be far better to talk about your problem with someone.

enough – must be used after an adjective or adverb

> He couldn't walk fast enough.

NOTES:

Be sure not to confuse adverbs of degree with adverbs of time, such as "just," "soon," "still," and "yet."

Adverbs of time indicate when something was done, rather than the intensity.

Now try the exercises on the next page.

Exercises – Adverbs of Degree

Put one of the adverbs of degree in the following sentences. Some sentences may have more than one correct answer. The answers to these exercises are provided at the back of the book.

absolutely / almost / barely / far / enough / even / hardly / nearly / quite

1) This jacket isn't big _____ for me.

2) You are _____ right about the situation.

3) In my opinion, pizza is _____ better than spaghetti.

4) He was _____ ready to go out; he only needed to put on his jacket.

5) He _____ fell off the edge of that cliff.

6) She was in serious condition at the hospital and _____ survived the accident.

7) We are _____ finished preparing the meal, so please sit at the table.

8) That old-fashioned dress can _____ be considered glamorous.

9) Your stupid remark wasn't _____ funny.

10) That outfit is _____ nice, but I prefer the other one.

Another / Other / Others

SINGLUAR ADJECTIVES

"Another" and "other" are adjectives and are singular.

Look at these examples:

> I would like another coffee, please.

"Another" is singular and modifies the noun "coffee."

> If the choice is between these two things, then I prefer the other one.

"Other" is an adjective and modifies "one" or "thing."

PLURAL PRONOUN

"Others" is a pronoun and is plural. "Other" can modify a plural noun.

Look at these examples:

> I like this painting, but there are many others in this museum.

"Others" is a plural pronoun which refers to the different paintings in the museum.

> Bill has three other sisters beside Berta.

"Other" is singular and modifies the noun "sisters."

USE AT END OF SENTENCE

"Another" and "other" can also be used at the end of a sentence, as shown in the following examples:

> He already has two dogs, but would still like another.

"Another" is singular, so in other words, he wants one more dog.

> Some people worry about health problems more than others.

"Others" is a plural pronoun that refers to other people.

Now try the exercises on the next page.

Exercises – Another / Other / Others

Complete the sentences with another, other, or others. The answers to these exercises are provided at the back of the book.

1) He has one house, but he wants to get _____ .

2) One student in the class wanted to go to a movie, but many _____ wanted to go bowling.

3) Some people like going to the beach more than _____ .

4) The family already has five adopted children, but would like _____ .

5) The choice so limited; I would prefer _____ options.

6) I had to decide between this jacket or the _____ one I have.

7) I like him, but _____ people don't like him so much.

8) I enjoy the rain, but _____ feel sad on rainy days.

9) James thought the book was great, but _____ friend of mine hated it.

10) Some people are more concerned than _____ about the potential tax increase.

Emphatic Form with Do and Did

We can use "do" or "did" with the base form of the verb to make a statement more emphatic.

Remember that the base form of the verb is the infinitive without "to."

Examples of the base form of the verb: see, eat, love, enjoy

The statement must always be in the affirmative.

DID – SPECIFIC ACTION OR EVENT IN THE PAST

We use the word "did" to emphasize a specific event or action that occurred in the past.

Examples:

> I know you think he couldn't have been at the party, but I *did see* him.
>
> I said I wouldn't touch the cake, but I *did eat* two pieces of it.

DO / DOES – GENERALIZATIONS OR SPECIFIC ACTION IN THE PRESENT

We use "do" or "does" for generalizations or to emphasize a specific event or action that occurs in the present.

Examples:

> In spite of having been told to be on time repeatedly, he still *does run* late on occasion.
>
> Even though I don't really like spinach, I *do eat* it sometimes.

The emphatic forms of the verbs are *highlighted* in the above sentences.

Notice that the other part of the sentence contains information that contradicts the statement made in the emphatic part.

Now try the exercises on the next page.

Exercises – Emphatic Form with Do and Did

Put the correct form of the verbs in the sentences provided below. One of the verbs must be in the emphatic form. The other verb may need to be in the negative form. The answers to these exercises are provided at the back of the book.

1) I thought he wouldn't want _____ (go) in the pool, but he _____ (swim).

2) Our boss has been told _____ (treat) his members of staff well, but he still _____ (insult) us from time to time.

3) You say you _____ (love) him anymore, but your actions show that you _____ (love) him.

4) You claim that you _____ (like) cake, but you _____ (eat) it sometimes.

5) In spite of _____ (leaving) very early, we _____ (arrive) late.

6) Even though she _____ (love) her children, she _____ (shout) at them terribly sometimes.

7) Although we _____ (repair) the car last week, it _____ (break down) again.

8) You claim _____ (be) indifferent to the situation, but you _____ (care) about it.

9) He pretends _____ (detest) tobacco use, but he _____ (smoke) almost every day.

10) She says that she _____ (have) any musical talent, but she _____ (sing) very well.

Modal Verbs

You may see questions on the grammar part of the test on modal verbs. Modal verbs are used to express obligation, certainty, possibility, or permission. Most commonly, the test assesses the modal verbs "should," "would," "might," and "could." However, sometimes other modal verbs such as "can," "may," or "must" are also included on the exam.

can

The modal verb "can" is used to show permission or possibility.

> A general possibility: Learning a language can be difficult.
>
> Permission: I can drive her car when she is out of town.

The word "can" is also used in passive sentence constructions, like in the examples below.

> Example – Active voice: You can declare that income on your tax return.
>
> Example – Passive voice: That income can be declared on your tax return.

could

The modal verb "could" is used to make suggestions and polite requests, as well as to talk about past possibilities and future possibilities.

> Suggestion: You could spend your holiday in Thailand.
>
> Polite request: Could I read that book when you have finished it?
>
> Past possibility: I could have failed the examination. I certainly hadn't studied enough for it.
>
> Future possibility: He could be found guilty of the crime when the police have finished their investigation.

may

The modal verb "may" is used to talk about present or future possibilities or to give permission.

> Present possibility: She may be upset right now, so I wouldn't tell her more bad news.
>
> Future possibility: She may be upset if you decide to lie to her.
>
> Permission: You may leave the table when you have finished eating.

might

The modal verb "might" is used to talk about future possibilities. It can also be used to talk about past possibilities.

> Future possibility: She might take a taxi home since the party is going to finish late.
>
> Past possibility: I might have failed the driving test. I certainly didn't feel prepared.

must

The modal verb "must" is used to express certainty or necessity.

> Certainty: That must have been the restaurant. It's the only one on the street.
>
> Necessity (for something that is necessary): You must have a valid library card to check out a book.

should

The word "should" is used to give advice or to express expectation or obligation. "Should" needs to be used with another verb.

> Advice: You should study hard for your exam.
>
> Expectation: You should be able to finish the work within three days.
>
> Obligation: You should have returned the video on time. Now you will have to pay a late fee.

would

The modal verb "would" can be used to express one's thoughts on an action in the past. Be sure to avoid the "would of" construction, which is not grammatical.

> CORRECT: I would have studied more if I had known the exam was going to be so difficult.
>
> INCORRECT: I would of studied more if I had known the exam was going to be so difficult.

The correct sentence above containing "would" is an example of the third conditional sentence structure.

Now try the exercises on the next page.

Exercises – Modal Verbs

Complete the following sentences, placing modal verbs in the space provided. Some sentences may have more than one answer. The answers to these exercises are provided at the back of the book.

1) You _____ have told us you weren't coming. We waited for over an hour. OBLIGATION

2) There are several ways to get to Boston from here. You _____ even take the train. SUGGESTION

3) Paloma said she _____ / _____ / _____ be going to the picnic tomorrow. She wasn't sure. FUTURE POSSIBILITY

4) You have a terrible cough. You _____ go to the doctor. ADVICE

5) He _____ have gone out for the night. He's not answering the phone. CERTAINTY

6) _____ / _____ / _____ I have another slice of cake, please? PERMISSION (2) / POLITE REQUEST (1)

7) The weather forecast said it _____ / _____ / _____ rain tomorrow. FUTURE POSSIBILITY

8) A good mother _____ / _____ always be concerned with the welfare of her children. NECESSITY (1) / ADVICE (1)

9) All residents _____ pay taxes if they have an income – it's the law. NECESSITY

10) What an awful accident. We _____ / _____ have been killed. PAST POSSIBILITY

Perfect Infinitive

The perfect infinitive is often assessed on the grammar part of the LOEP Test.

It is formed as follows: verb + to + has / have + past participle

Usage with Common Verbs

The perfect infinitive is often used after the following words:

claim, expect, hate, hope, like, love, want, pretend

Look at these examples:

> She claimed to have lost her phone when we were out last week.
>
> He pretended to have decided what to do, although I knew he hadn't.

Past Usage

As in the examples above, the perfect infinitive often refers to events that have taken place in the past.

Look at more examples:

> I feel privileged to have worked here for the past five years.
>
> He was lucky enough to have lived in Paris.

Future Usage

The perfect infinitive can also refer to things that will take place in the future.

Look at these examples:

> We hope to have finished the job by the end of the month
>
> She wants to have lost five pounds before she goes on vacation.

Passive Form

The perfect infinitive also has a passive form.

The perfect infinitive passive is formed as follows:

> verb + to + has / have + + been + past participle

The passive form of the perfect infinitive is often used after the following words:

believe, said, claim, like, love, understand

Look at this example:

These caves are said to have been formed over millions of years.

Now try the exercises on the next page.

Exercises – Perfect Infinitive

Complete the sentences with the perfect infinitive form of the given verb. You may need to use either the active or the passive form. The answers to these exercises are provided at the back of the book.

1) I wanted _____ (wear) something better to the surprise party last night, but I had nothing else packed in my suitcase.

2) She claimed _____ (pass) her test, although he didn't believe her.

3) I pretended _____ (enjoy) myself after going to that party, but I really detested it.

4) I feel so lucky _____ (visit) London on vacation last year.

5) Some of our oldest laws are said _____ (influence) by those from ancient Greece.

6) He passed away recently, but I was happy _____ (know) him so well during his lifetime.

7) We hope _____ (win) the championship when we are on our way home from the tournament next week.

8) I feel fortunate _____ (love) by a wonderful spouse for forty years.

9) She hopes _____ (be) on her vacation for four days by this time next week.

10) The geological features are said _____ (change) over time by the flow of water in the area.

Pronouns in the Accusative Case

The pronoun "I" is in the nominative case and should be used as a grammatical subject.

You should use "I" last if you are naming more than one person in the grammatical subject.

> *Example:* Sung Li, Marta, and I went shopping last Wednesday.

The word "me" is in the accusative case and should be used as an object.

> *Example:* Tom emailed me yesterday.

MORE THAN ONE GRAMMATICAL OBJECT

Confusion sometimes occurs when more than one person is mentioned as the object of the sentence.

CORRECT: I told you to send Tom and me a copy of the letter.

INCORRECT: I told you to send Tom and I a copy of the letter.

AFTER PREPOSITIONS

Also be sure to use the accusative case after prepositions.

CORRECT: Between you and me, I'm not sure whether to believe her story.

INCORRECT: Between you and I, I'm not sure whether to believe her story.

OTHER PRONOUNS

The same rules apply to he / him, she / her, they / them, and we / us.

> *Example:* Sung Li, Marta, and she went shopping last Wednesday.
>
> I told you to send a copy of the letter to Tom and him.
>
> I told you to send a copy of the letter to them and us

Now try the exercises on the next page.

Exercises – Pronouns in the Accusative Case

Put the correct form of the pronoun in the gaps in the sentences below. The answers to these exercises are provided at the back of the book.

1) He doesn't want to get involved because this problem is between you and _____ (first person).

2) That issue needs to be discussed at a meeting with all of you and _____ (second person masculine).

3) The tour of the factory for you and _____ (first person) will take place at 9:00 AM tomorrow.

4) If you had wanted to speak to her, you should have said something when you and _____ (third person feminine) were together yesterday.

5) Because we weren't invited to his party, he didn't get a birthday present from either _____ (third person feminine) or _____ (first person).

6) I don't want to argue with you or _____. (third person masculine)

7) He wants to give the instructions to her, you, and _____ (first person) all together in order to save time.

8) In case you need something else from us, just call either _____ (third person feminine) or _____ . (first person)

9) I simply couldn't believe her after all of the lies she has told you and _____ (first person).

10) She seems to hold something against us because you and _____ (first person) got better grades than she did.

Pronouns – Demonstrative and Relative Pronouns

DEMONSTRATIVE PRONOUNS

Demonstrative pronouns include the following words: this, that, these, those

This / That

"This" is used for a singular item that is nearby. "That" is used for singular items that are further away in time or space.

Singular: This book that I have here is really interesting.

Plural: That book on the table over there is really interesting.

These / Those

"These" is used for plural items that are nearby. "Those" is used for plural items that are further away in time or space.

Singular: These pictures on my phone were taken on our vacation.

Plural: Those pictures on the wall were taken on our vacation.

Avoid using "them" instead of "those":

INCORRECT: Them pictures on the wall were taken on our vacation.

RELATIVE PRONOUNS

Relative pronouns include the following: which, that, who, whom, whose

"Which" and "that" are used to describe things, and "who" and "whom" are used to describe people. "Whose" is used for people or things.

Which / That / Who

WHICH: Last night, I watched a romantic-comedy movie which was really funny.

THAT: Last night, I watched a romantic-comedy movie that was really funny.

WHO: Susan always remains calm under pressure, unlike Tom, who is always so nervous.

"Who" is used because we are describing the person. This is known as the nominative case.

Whom / Whose

WHOM: To whom should the report be given?

"Whom" is used because the person is receiving an action, which is receiving the report. This is known as the accusative case.

WHOSE: I went out for lunch with Marta, whose parents are from Costa Rica.

WHOSE: I went out for lunch yesterday at that new restaurant, whose name I don't remember.

Now try the exercises on the next page.

Exercises – Demonstrative and Relative Pronouns

Complete the sentences with the following words: this, that, these, those, that, which, who, whom, whose. Some sentences may have more than one answer. The answers to these exercises are provided at the back of the book.

1) Last night, I read a graphic novel _____ was really interesting.

2) She has only one sister, _____ lives in Los Angeles.

3) _____ magazine, _____ I have here in my hand, is so boring.

4) _____ day last week was one of the worst days of my life.

5) His brother, _____ name is Samuel, is studying to become a lawyer.

6) I need to wear _____ gloves in the closet upstairs when I go out.

7) If you would like to know what my daughter looks like, have a look at _____ pictures right here.

8) I wanted to deliver the project, but I wasn't informed to _____ it should be given.

9) That city, _____ name I can't remember, is on the border of Kansas and Missouri.

10) She told everyone my secret, _____ really annoyed me.

REVIEW OF VERB USAGE AND TENSE

ACTIVE VOICE

Present simple tense

The present simple tense is used for habitual actions.

> Example: He goes to the office at 8:00 every morning.

The present tense is also used to state facts or generalizations.

> Example: Water freezes at zero degrees Celsius.

The present simple tense is formed as follows:

- I work.
- You work.
- He / She / It works.
- We work.
- You work. (Plural)
- They work.

Past simple tense

The past simple tense is used for actions that were started and completed in the past.

> Example: I walked three miles yesterday.

The past simple tense is formed as follows:

- I worked.
- You worked.
- He / She / It worked.
- We worked.
- You worked. (Plural)
- They worked.

Please note that the previous example contains the regular verb "work." You should also be acquainted with the irregular verb forms for the exam.

Future simple tense

The future simple tense is used for actions that will occur in the future.

>Example: Jane will study in the evening tomorrow.

The future simple tense is formed as follows:

- I will work.
- You will work.
- He / She / It will work.
- We will work.
- You will work. (Plural)
- They will work.

Simple tenses:
Present simple – habits, truths, or generalizations
Past simple – actions completed in the past
Future simple – actions to be completed in the future

Present perfect tense

The present perfect tense is used for actions that were completed in the past, but that have relevancy in the present time.

>Example: I have studied every day this week.

The phrase "this week" shows that the action has relevancy in the present time.

The present perfect tense is formed as follows:

- I have worked.
- You have worked.
- He / She / It has worked.
- We have worked.

- You have worked. (Plural)
- They have worked.

Past perfect tense

The past perfect is often used for an action which has just recently occurred.

The past perfect form can also be used to show that one action preceded another when a sentence describes two past actions. In this situation, the past perfect is used for the action which happened first. The simple past is used for the subsequent action.

The past perfect is often used with the words "just" and "after" and with the phrase "no sooner . . . than."

>Example: I had just finished writing her an email when she called me.

There are two actions in the above sentence, but the action of writing was finished before the action of calling.

Remember that the auxiliary verb must come before the word "just."

>Example: We had just arrived, when she decided to leave.

"No sooner" is a negative adverbial. Accordingly, the auxiliary verb needs to be inverted in sentences that have this adverbial phrase.

>Example: No sooner had we arrived, than she decided to leave.

The past perfect tense is formed as follows:

- I had worked.
- You had worked.
- He / She / It had worked.
- We had worked.
- You had worked. (Plural)
- They had worked.

Future perfect tense

The future perfect tense is used to describe an action that will be completed at a definite time in the future.

> Example: By this time next week, I will have finished all of my exams.

The future perfect tense is formed as follows:

- I will have worked.
- You will have worked.
- He / She / It will have worked.
- We will have worked.
- You will have worked. (Plural)
- They will have worked.

Perfect tenses:
Present perfect – actions completed in the past, but relevant in the present time
Past perfect – an action in the past that is relevant in the present and was completed before another action in the past
Future perfect – actions to be completed by a specific time in the future

---

Present simple progressive

The present simple progressive is used to describe actions that are in progress at the time of speaking.

> Example: He is studying for his final exams right now.

The present simple progressive is also used to describe actions that will take place at a fixed time in the future.

> Example: He is leaving for London on Tuesday.

The present simple progressive is formed as follows:

- I am working.
- You are working.
- He / She / It is working.

- We are working.
- You are working. (Plural)
- They are working.

Past simple progressive

The past simple progressive is used for actions that were in progress in the past.

The past simple progressive can be used to indicate that an action was in progress in the past when it was interrupted by a subsequent action.

> Example: I was cleaning the house yesterday when the doorbell rang.

The past simple progressive is formed as follows:

- I was working.
- You were working.
- He / She / It was working.
- We were working.
- You were working. (Plural)
- They were working.

Future simple progressive

The future simple progressive is used for actions that will be in progress in the future.

> Example: Jane will be traveling around the world next year.

The future simple tense is formed as follows:

- I will be working.
- You will be working.
- He / She / It will be working.
- We will be working.
- You will be working. (Plural)
- They will be working.

Present perfect progressive

The present perfect progressive is used for actions that were in progress in the past, but that have relevancy in the present time.

> Example: I have been working very hard lately.

The phrase "lately" shows that the action has relevancy in the present time.

The present perfect progressive is formed as follows:

- I have been working.
- You have been working.
- He / She / It has been working.
- We have been working.
- You have been working. (Plural)
- They have been working.

Progressive forms:
Present simple progressive – action is in progress at the time of speaking or is to take place at a definite time in the future
Past simple progressive – actions in progress in the past
Future simple progressive – actions to be in progress in the future

---

PASSIVE VOICE

Use the passive voice to emphasize the object of the action, rather than the person doing the action or the action itself.

In the example sentences that follow in this section, the diplomas are the object of the action. We want to emphasize the fact that the diplomas are being issued. We want to de-emphasize the fact that the university officials are the people responsible for handing out the diplomas.

In other words, we could write our example sentence in the active voice, like this:

>Example (Active voice): The university officials hand out diplomas on graduation day every year.

Present simple passive

The present simple passive describes generalizations or things that normally occur in a predictable way.

>Example: Diplomas are handed out on graduation day every year.

Past simple passive

The past simple passive is used to show that an action was completed in the past.

>Example: Diplomas were handed out on graduation day last year.

Future simple passive

The future simple passive is used for events that will be completed in the future.

>Example: Diplomas will be handed out on graduation day in May this year.

Future passive with is / are

The "future passive with is / are" is used in the sentence below because it describes an action that is planned for the future.

>Example: Diplomas are to be handed out on graduation day in May this year.

Present simple progressive passive

The present simple progressive passive is used in the sentence below because we are talking about an action that will take place during a definite time in the future. This form emphasizes that a plan is in place for the event.

>Example: Diplomas are being handed out on graduation day, which is May 18th this year.

Past simple progressive passive

The past simple progressive passive is used to show that an action was in progress in the past, and we want to put an emphasis on that action.

> Example: The diplomas were being handed out on graduation day when the ceremony was interrupted.

Present perfect passive

The present perfect passive is used in the sentence below because it emphasizes that the diplomas have been handed out like this in the past, and this action continues in the present.

> Example: Diplomas have been handed out on graduation day since the university was founded in 1924.

Past perfect passive

The past perfect passive is used in the following sentence because it emphasizes that the diplomas were handed out like this in the past, but the policy on handing out diplomas in this way has recently changed.

> Example: Diplomas had been handed out on graduation day until last year, when they started to be sent in the mail.

Now try the three sets of grammar review exercises on the following pages.

GRAMMAR REVIEW EXERCISES – SET 1

1. I don't know _____ the promotion or not.
   A. whether got
   B. he got
   C. if he got
   D. that he got

2. Paveen was elated because she saw her parents, who _____ their anniversary last week.
   A. were celebrating
   B. had celebrated
   C. has celebrated
   D. celebrate

3. Someone once told me _____ to Canada in the winter.
   A. not to travel
   B. not traveling
   C. not travel
   D. if I not travel

4. _____ in watching classic movies.
   A. I am interesting
   B. Interesting it is
   C. I am interested
   D. It is interesting

5. That phone has an application _____ videos.
   A. by which plays
   B. which are plays
   C. by which are plays
   D. which plays

6. _____ spaghetti only once since I arrived in Italy.
   A. I have eaten
   B. Did I eat
   C. Have I eaten
   D. I ate

7. The problems from last year _____ their toll on her.
   A. taken
   B. have taken
   C. made
   D. have made

8. You would have passed your test _____ more.
   A. had you studied
   B. if you studied
   C. you had studied
   D. would you studied

9. That store has clothes that aren't _____ elsewhere.
   A. to be sold
   B. selling
   C. sold
   D. to sell

10. _____ been there, I can't really say if I like Los Angeles.
    A. Never having
    B. Never had
    C. Never to have
    D. Never to

11. She would have _____ in the accident had she not put on her seat belt.
    A. injury
    B. been injuring
    C. been injured
    D. to be injured

12. To _____ a long story short, I decided not to go to Los Angeles.
    A. take
    B. make
    C. taking
    D. making

13. People _____ about that new video.
    A. constant talk
    B. constant talking
    C. constantly to be talking
    D. are constantly talking

14. He was evicted from his apartment, but what _____ was pay his rent on time.
    A. he should do
    B. should he do
    C. he should have done
    D. he should be doing

15. The professor was telling us not _____ so much time talking.
    A. spending
    B. to be spending
    C. to spending
    D. be spending

GRAMMAR REVIEW EXERCISES – SET 2

1. We don't have any plans for tonight. How about _____ bowling?
    A. to go
    B. we go
    C. going for
    D. going

2. Teachers get tired of students _____ about how much homework they are given.
    A. to complain
    B. complaints
    C. to have complained
    D. complaining

3. If you want to go for a hamburger, I _____ one too.
    A. like to have
    B. feel like to have
    C. feel like having
    D. feel like I have had

4. The new fitness center _____ next week.
    A. be opening
    B. is being opening
    C. will opening
    D. is having its opening

5. Janet told me about the surprise party, although she _____ .
    A. mightn't have
    B. won't have
    C. shouldn't have
    D. couldn't have

6. I have seen one of Monet's paintings in a museum, but I _____ .
    A. from where can't remember
    B. where can't remember
    C. can't remember from where
    D. can't remember where

7. I'm glad you _____ me that you had already completed the report.
   A. had told
   B. told
   C. were telling
   D. tell

8. That presentation was far too advanced _____ as an introductory lecture.
   A. to be suiting
   B. for suiting
   C. to be suitable
   D. suitably

9. He is _____ his friends.
   A. shorter of
   B. the shortest
   C. shorter than
   D. shortest of

10. I really regret _____ harder to increase my savings.
    A. not having tried
    B. not to try
    C. not to tried
    D. not to trying

11. She _____ me to loan her some money last month.
    A. had asked
    B. asked
    C. has been asking
    D. had been asking

12. We couldn't have completed the project without Ahmed, who _____ a great deal of expertise to the team.
    A. brought
    B. had brought
    C. will have brought
    D. will be bringing

13. Once he _____ that he wasn't going to be able to go to college, he felt a lot better.
    A. accepts
    B. did accept
    C. will accept
    D. had accepted

14. She was upset about not receiving an invitation; we _____ have invited her.
    A. must
    B. may
    C. should
    D. ought

15. Your monetary compensation agreement is in the envelope _____ was forwarded to your attorney.
    A. which
    B. in which
    C. where
    D. in that

GRAMMAR REVIEW EXERCISES – SET 3

1. I expect her _____ out of her parents' house now that she has finished college.
   A. to move
   B. moving
   C. being moved
   D. to have been moving

2. This isn't my first draft of the assignment; I _____ it.
   A. had yet re-written
   B. re-wrote already
   C. have already re-written
   D. re-written already

3. He's getting married tomorrow, and _____ him so worried.
   A. never have I seen
   B. never I saw
   C. I have seen never
   D. I saw never

4. Perhaps she _____ stay home than go shopping with us.
   A. might better
   B. would rather
   C. much better
   D. could rather

5. He gets _____ grades of all the students in his class.
   A. the best
   B. the better
   C. the best of
   D. better than

6. Just after we _____ , he decided to leave.
   A. had arrived
   B. have arrived
   C. are arriving
   D. were arrived

7. The teacher told me off _____ to class.
   A. to be late
   B. to being late
   C. for being late
   D. being late

8. I'm sure that _____ to Disneyland will be a lot of fun.
   A. to go
   B. going
   C. to be going
   D. having gone

9. In addition to _____ , Darnell also enjoys watching movies.
   A. hike
   B. he hikes
   C. hiking
   D. he hiking

10. I am enjoying my new apartment now that I have gotten used _____ the neighborhood.
    A. to walking around
    B. walking around
    C. to walk around
    D. walk around

11. _____ my best friend only once since she moved to Minneapolis.
    A. I have seen
    B. Did I see
    C. Have I seen
    D. I saw

12. The teacher actually suggested a solution that I already had thought _____ .
    A. to be done
    B. to do
    C. to doing
    D. of doing

13. I knew that it was time we _____ the party. It was getting so late.
    A. leave
    B. left
    C. had left
    D. were leaving

14. The new supermarket is believed _____ next week.
    A. be closing
    B. to be closing
    C. it is closing
    D. to having its closing

15. That problem is between you and _____; you shouldn't discuss it with anyone else.
    A. I
    B. me
    C. mine
    D. my

ANSWERS TO THE BONUS EXERCISES

Adverbs of Location

1) anyplace / anywhere

2) elsewhere / somewhere else / another place

3) everywhere

4) anyplace else / anywhere else

5) somewhere

6) anyplace / anywhere

7) elsewhere / somewhere else / to another place

8) somewhere

9) anywhere else / anyplace else

10) everywhere

Adverbs of Degree

1) enough

2) absolutely

3) far

4) almost / nearly

5) almost / nearly

6) barely

7) almost / nearly

8) hardly

9) even

10) quite

Another / Other / Others

1) another

2) others

3) others

4) others, another

5) other

6) other

7) other

8) others

9) another

10) others

Emphatic Form (Do and Did)

1) to go, did swim

2) to treat, does insult

3) don't love, do love

4) don't like, do eat

5) leaving / having left, did arrive

6) loves, does shout

7) repaired, did break down

8) to be, do care

9) to detest, does smoke

10) doesn't have, does sing

Modal Verbs

1) should

2) could

3) could, may, might

4) should

5) must

6) may, can, could

7) may, might, could

8) must, should

9) must

10) could, might

Perfect Infinitive

1) to have worn

2) to have passed

3) to have enjoyed

4) to have visited

5) to have been influenced

6) to have known

7) to have won

8) to have been loved

9) to have been

10) to have been changed

Pronouns in the Accusative Case

1) me

2) him

3) me

4) she

5) her, me

6) him

7) me

8) her, me

9) me

10) I

Pronouns – Demonstrative and Relative Pronouns

1) which, that

2) who

3) This, which

4) That

5) whose

6) those

7) these

8) whom

9) whose

10) which

Grammar Review Exercises – Set 1

1) C

2) A

3) A

4) C

5) D

6) A

7) B

8) A

9) C

10) A

11) C

12) B

13) D

14) C

15) B

Grammar Review Exercises – Set 2

1) D

2) D

3) C

4) D

5) C

6) D

7) B

8) C

9) C

10) A

11) B

12) A

13) D

14) C

15) A

Grammar Review Exercises – Set 3

1) A

2) C

3) A

4) B

5) A

6) A

7) C

8) B

9) C

10) A

11) A

12) D

13) B

14) B

15) B

www.ingramcontent.com/pod-product-compliance
Lightning Source LLC
Chambersburg PA
CBHW081749100526
44592CB00015B/2350